Grief Thoughts

Brief Anecdotes About Profound Loss

ISSA M. MAS

Grief Thoughts

© 2021 Issa M. Mas

ISBN 978-1-66781-037-9
eBook ISBN 978-1-66781-038-6

For Theo,
to whom I owe more than I could ever repay.

Prologue

Leonardo (Lenny) Mas was many things, all of them layered and complicated. He spent his life wanting to protect the world from the "bad guys," having spent his childhood living with the worst bad guy of all, his own father. Despite experiencing horrific child abuse he swore he'd do things differently with his own child, and that he did. For the most part. Being the child of a child abuse survivor is a unique blend of inheriting dysfunction, and if you're lucky, being grateful things were nowhere near as bad for you as they were for them because they worked so hard to break the cycle. In many ways he did break the cycle, and, alas, in some ways he couldn't help but to perpetuate the impossibly exacting standards that was the scaffold of his painful relationship with his father.

My job, especially since his passing, has been to balance out the ways in which his upbringing inadvertently harmed me, with the ways his devotion to me consistently provided protection, support, pride, and so much love. This book is dedicated to those who grieve complicated people. We cannot and should not canonize them in their absence, because healing lies within truth. We cannot and should not vilify them either, because the truth is that they tried so very hard, and for that they should be honored.

1

Fuck Today

As a child and young adult, my dad discouraged me as an artist. Whether it was singing or writing, creativity was a thing to enjoy as a hobby but not solid enough to build a life upon. He felt strongly that his job as a father was to make sure I was capable of having a viable, stable career that would utilize my intellectual gifts and provide me with the financial means to live a successful life as a self-sufficient woman. It was loving and responsible. It made perfect sense. It broke my heart. It fractured my wings.

Then one day, after two weeks in the ICU, then several weeks of general hospitalization, then two weeks of rehab to relearn how to walk again, my dad finally came home three days before my birthday — and do you know what he did for that birthday? He handed me an envelope with enough money to not work for 6 months and said, "Write. I know it's what you love. Go write."

I didn't get to use that time to write because I used all of that time to advocate for his best possible care as his health care proxy. Months of oncology visits and radiation appointments and chemotherapy appointments. Of researching and explaining medical terms to his anxiety-addled brain. Months of arguing with him, comforting his fears, and trying and failing to comfort my own. Four months and one day later he was gone. That's all the time I got with him. Six years ago today.

So. Here I am. Writing. Yet again.

And yes — that *is* a grapefruit mimosa on my desk next to my computer. Because fuck today.

2

Grief Thoughts

He lost consciousness at home with his sister. The ambulance has taken him to the hospital. I'm on my way there. They won't tell me what's going on over the phone. Please pray?

3

He's gone.

1

I woke up today a fatherless child.

5

The image of my 8-year-old son trying to be stoic by hiding his face from me so that I didn't see his sadness when I told him his grandpa was gone . . .

The feeling of his little hand rubbing my back and his little kiss on my forehead . . .

The sound of my child's voice, sounding smaller than I've heard it sound in years, saying, "I love you, Mama . . ."

These are some of the ways my heart broke today.

Nobody ever tells you that there are a million little ways your heart can break.

Nobody ever tells you that your heart can break anew while in the midst of it already breaking.

Nobody ever tells you that the price of love is grief.

6

I am about to purchase something for my son and I to wear to my father's funeral. That is the most surreal fucking sentence I've ever written in my entire life.

7

The doorbell just rang and my kid said, "Oooh! Who's that; Grandpa?!?"

"Oh. Wait. Never mind."

I can't do this . . .

8

If one more person says, "But, you have to write his eulogy, you're a writer!" I'm going to stab myself with a quill dipped in cyanide. I don't even know how I'm going to walk into that building, much less go up and speak words. It's not about what I might regret later, it's about not ending up in a hospital right now so that I can be here for my kid during this soul-devouring time. Every time I think of what I could possibly write my heart screams so loud my head hurts. My eulogy, my testimony to him as a human being and as a father, will be the continued embodiment of all he taught me. Right now the fact that my brain hasn't broken down along with my heart is victory enough.

9

I can't think, I can't breathe, I can't walk, I can't sit, I can't read, I can't listen to music. I can't look at my child, I can't watch TV, I can't seem to do one single goddamn thing without "DADDY IS DEAD" reverberating through my skull.

I have no idea how I'm going to get through this.

10

On top of everything I've been through the last three weeks I am also single again now.

That piece of trash was sleeping with his co-worker as I tended to my ailing father.

How could someone do that? How could someone see how hard I was fighting to keep my father alive and decide I wasn't "spending enough time focused on him?" What kind of monster does that to someone they say they care about? To someone they say they *loved*?

My heart. If it weren't for my kid I don't know that it could keep beating anymore. It's been through more than I feel I can bear.

It's too much.

It's too fucking much!

11

Do you ever get post-breakup Tourette's? Like, you're humming along, minding your own business, doing laundry, and all of a sudden you remember something that makes you so angry you burst forth with a, "That BASTARD!" but then you just continue folding your kid's undershirts, glad that said kid is in the living room and didn't hear you?

No?

Ok.

. . . never mind . . .

12

A month ago today. A month ago from right now I was racing to Brooklyn praying that I would make it in time. A month ago today I got to the hospital and saw my daddy, dead, on a hospital gurney. It's been an entire month. Why does it feel like it all just happened yesterday? I can't seem to move forward. I'm so stuck here. I was supposed to have accomplished so much in this month on his behalf for his estate and I've literally accomplished nothing. Not one thing. I take my kid to school and then I go back home and climb into bed and just lie there and Netflix. Then I get up and pick him up from school and take good care of him, and after I put him to bed at night I climb back into my own bed again. I've lost my father, then my partner, and what feels like most of my sanity this last month. All I can think to do is to reach out to the people who love me and ask, "I know you're probably tired of praying for me, I realize that I've been a giant energy suck this year, but if you could pray that I find my way through this grief into healing I would be beyond grateful."

It's literally all I can think to do right now.

13

My therapist said she wishes we could all go back to a time when mourners wore all black for up to a year, because then at least their grief was visible and respected. People knew to not ask too much of mourners, to excuse a certain amount of erratic behavior, to be extra kind and easier on them, to show them compassion. She said that modern society's predilection for going back to work the very next day after the death of a loved one, this pervasive obsession with being unnaturally stoic, was a "precarious kind of strong," and was, in her personal and professional opinion, often mentally unhealthy. She said the practice of dressing in all black, veil included, was a gift to the mourner and the mourner's community, and it's a pity we don't do that anymore.

As a New Yorker I spend most of my time dressed in black anyway, but it was the sentiment that moved me. She understood me completely.

Now I need to figure out how to rock a veil with black jeans.

14

It was only seven weeks ago today. Every Monday I count how many weeks it's been. There are still times each and every day that I reach for my phone when something happens and I want to tell him. Then it hits me.

"Shit. I can't call him. He's dead."

At least it was Mondays his death ruined. Like, "I already didn't like you, Monday, but I can't fucking stand your ass now."

Better than losing Friday, my favorite day. Monday was already an asshole to begin with.

15

Sometimes I think of who I could be and all I could've accomplished by now if I hadn't spent most of my energy over the past twenty years fighting major depression and it breaks my fucking heart. Now I've been broken by grief as well, and I feel like the progress I was making in therapy and other personal growth work has all been dashed against jagged rocks at the bottom of the cliff of my mourning.

I can't seem to stay out of bed most days. Oh, I get up and make my kid his breakfast and make sure he gets dressed and brushes his teeth. I walk him to school and smile at the teachers and the other parents and play along like I'm not dying inside. The second I'm back at home, though, I crawl back into bed and stay there until it's time to pick him up again. Sometimes I nap. Sometimes I make up for not being able to sleep the night before. Mostly I just lie there and check out. I watch Netflix or scroll through social media wrapped in my blankets like a human grief burrito. I do nothing but exist. I do nothing but hurt. I don't see an end to this, and that scares the shit out of me.

Be kind, y'all. You really have no idea what the person next to you is going through. If you have the ability to choose whether to be right or to be kind, choose kindness. Your "right" actually might not be as right as you believe it to be. Be kind. Be love.

16

Mothers are seldom given the right to express that the joy which often keeps them going when things are at their most bleak — their children — can also at times be a source of resentment when you feel stuck in a role you'd never actually choose to abdicate. The Cult of Motherhood doesn't just ask for your blood, your sweat, and your tears; it often asks for a facade of faultlessness to be perpetuated, behind which most mothers lament their inability to get anywhere close to the perfection showcased on Pinterest boards or HGTV.

Here's to the mothers who know better, who thumb their noses at convention and flip the bird at patriarchal ideals of June Cleaver-esque motherhood. Come, sit by me; I have pizza. And no, it's not handmade with local, artisanal ingredients, but I live in New York City and nobody's pizza is better than ours.

The wine is from France, though. I do have great taste.

17

I just saw a mouse and let out a shriek, and then I yelled, "GET OUT OF MY HOUSE YOU STUPID MOUSE! I HATE YOU!"

My kid: Mama! Don't say that!

Me: Why not? IT'S A STUPID MOUSE AND I HATE IT!

Him: Mama! You can't say that! What if it's Grandpa and he already reincarnated and he's that mouse? You'll hurt his feelings!

Filed under: Things Buddhist Kids Say

18

My kid just got out of bed and came to me saying he felt something like a wet kiss on his head, and asked if I thought it was Grandpa.

I nodded and said, "Probably; yes."

Now I'm hiding in the bathroom, sobbing. Trying to tell myself it's only been 2 months and 6 days, falling apart every now and then is perfectly normal.

And by normal I mean I hate this shit.

I fucking hate it.

19

I don't know how to exist in a world where my father no longer does.

20

I just used the last paper towel of the huge economy pack my dad got us. I'm standing here over the kitchen sink holding a cardboard tube, fighting back the urge to break down and cry, because I just used the last paper towel he bought me. This is the sheer insanity of grief.

21

Pay attention to the people who protest when you start making yourself an actual priority in your own life. Pay attention to the ways they point out how "you've changed" or "you're overreacting" when you no longer allow a lack of reciprocity on their part in your relationship with them, especially as you process profound grief. Pay attention to those who would rather you be weak and fragile, even as you are curled up into a ball on your bed for the fourth day in a row, instead of strong and steady, despite your excruciating pain. You can be strong and steady while grieving. You can be strong and steady while falling apart. Pay attention to those who view how you process this grief in unapologetic ways as weakness. Pay close attention.

22

Although my dad and I were very close, it's challenging to grieve for a complicated parent. He was a pain in the ass, my old man. Our relationship was difficult and tumultuous. It was fraught with misunderstandings and heated arguments. We fought ferociously, but we loved each other so deeply — and consistently showed it — that I am sure in my very soul we have loved each other for millennia; each reincarnation finding us in each other's lives again. I sometimes dream of reincarnating as his mother in the next life so that I can give him all the love, kindness, and protection he never received as a child in this lifetime. Maybe we'll get it "right" in our next life. I hope so. For now I walk around feeling as if I am missing a limb.

23

When you're in Starbucks and someone orders a Holiday Flat White and you have to physically restrain yourself from yelling, "HOLIDAY FLAT WHITE IS PEOPLE!!!" but you know nobody will get the joke and you'll just get carted off to a rubber room. Then you reach for your phone because you know your dad would've found it funny since he actually saw *Soylent Green* in the movie theater when it first came out, and all of a sudden the chuckle dries out on your lips and you have to fight tears in public. Yet again.

29

My kid: Mama, if you got a magic wish ring and you could wish for anything in the world, what would it be?

Him, before I could even answer: Oh, I know what it would be. You'd wish for Grandpa back, right?

I nodded yes, but all I could think of was *The Monkey's Paw*.

Related: Did you know that 3:42 pm is the perfect time for a glass of Pinot Noir?

25

I had plans to get up at my normal early time and go to the gym, then come home and tackle the immense amount of cleaning I have to do around here while my kid is away for the weekend. So far, the only thing I've managed to do was go back to sleep and just wake up. Part of me feels like a failure, while the other part is wondering what I can order for breakfast from the diner. The cleaning will have to wait a little longer. The stress of the last few months has been so overwhelming, and my body is clearly telling me I need the rest, so I'm going to listen to it instead of listening to the judgmental task master who lives in my head.

She wants the house clean so badly she can do it herself.

26

I had all these plans for today, including two different holiday parties this evening, and all I've been able to do is sit around on my sofa and watch ghost stories all day.

Yes, obviously I'm working through my grief in some weird, "let me watch movies about dead people coming back from the grave" sort of way.

He loved everything supernatural, and my love of creepy stuff comes from him. At some point I realized that I'm mad at him for not visiting me. I thought for sure I would've seen him around the house by now. I feel completely abandoned.

Yes, I'm aware of how insane I sound. I've only had one glass of wine, don't worry. Gonna make myself a Coke float now and maybe have some cake for dinner. That should complete tonight's feeling of my being a lost child.

27

All day I kept thinking, "I have to call Dad and wish him a Merry Christmas," and then I'd remember.

Over and over and fucking over again.

I'm so tired.

28

Managing the grief over my father's death while simultaneously processing the end of my romantic relationship has been a real trip, and I've realized something. You could have a ton in common with your significant other. You can both like art house films, 60s jazz, and international restaurants, but if your demons don't play nice together, the relationship probably won't work. And by "relationship" I mean both romantic and platonic ones.

See, everyone's got demons. We all have our issues, our short-comings, our emotional wounds and/or blockages. We're human, and even the most self-actualized among us have spaces in us that stem from a place of trauma or inner darkness — a place of "lack," a place of "not good enough." Some have very few, some have legions, but we all have our demons.

Now, if your demons play nicely with one another, you could have absolutely zero in common. You could like 80s soundtrack pop and they could like 90s New Jack Swing R&B. You could like independent documentaries and they could like Hollywood action blockbusters. You can itch just at the thought of stepping foot inside a park and they could adore going camping most weekends. It doesn't matter. If your demons play nice, your relationship will work and no one will understand how you've managed to stay together for so long. It's because your demons are not constantly trying to rip each other apart and establish complete and total dominance over their little corner of Hell.

When your demons aren't constantly in life's school playground trying to shank each other with homemade shivs, you can access the love and respect that's to be found in your relationship, regardless of the particulars that make each of you individuals. When your demons are out in these relationship streets trying to slice each other up, no matter how much your heart sees the potential and wishes things were different, you'll always be doing battle, and find nothing but pain and exhaustion in your relationship. It's not about how much you have in common with someone, nor about how many of the "dream qualities" a person has, or how good they are "on paper." Do your demons play nicely with each other? Do they live and let live, or do they constantly try to negatively trigger and/or take each other out?

Look at the ways in which you at your worst, and your partner at their worst, relate. If your demons can, at the very least, do no harm to one another, you're already ahead of the game. If not, sometimes all you can do is get an exorcism of that person and their demons; especially if they won't take responsibility for their inner wounds and how they show up in relation to others.

This was just another huge lesson I learned last year. The hits just kept coming.

29

I never understood that whole "being mad at someone for passing away" thing. It never made sense to me. Being sad — yes, of course. Feeling a profound sense of loss, definitely. But being mad at them for dying? That made no real sense to me.

I'm fucking pissed.

I'm so goddamn ANGRY. I'm angry at him! I'M ANGRY AT HIM FOR LEAVING US. I'M FUCKING FURIOUS AT HIM FOR ABANDONING US. HOW FUCKING DARE HE?!? Wasn't I a good enough daughter? Didn't I take his shit and love him regardless of it my WHOLE FUCKING LIFE? Why the FUCK did he give up? Why did he leave us in such a mess and why didn't he protect us from his evil fucking siblings, who stole all the things he specifically left for me and my kid and fled the city? WHY DID HE LEAVE ME ALL ALONE IN THIS WORLD? HOW COULD HE LEAVE HIS GRAND BABY??? HOW COULD HE FUCKING DO THIS TO US???

(Okay. This concludes my hysterical breakdown for the day. Back to trying to act like I'm "normal.")

30

Hey, random man on the street with a cough that sounded so exactly like my father's that I almost gave myself whiplash when I spun my head around to look at who was making that sound: thank you for making my heart crack open and bleed into my chest cavity! Have a great day!

Ugh.

31

My dad was a man's man, possessed of very old school testoster-one-driven masculinity, and he once said of me, "The only person on this planet who has balls as big as mine is my daughter." HEH. It's an odd thing for a feminist to be thankful for, but I remember those words — words spoken by a man who ran into a building that people were running from screaming to save humans he did not know FOUR TIMES before he himself collapsed from smoke inhalation — when I feel like I can't take another step.

32

Woke up to a mouse caught in a trap in the kitchen and I have to wait for my Super to get here to remove it. I refuse to wake my kid up until the Super gets here because I'm not stepping foot in that kitchen to make his breakfast while it's in there squeaking. So, my kid's going to be late to school.

Because of a mouse.

So much for those balls my dad said I had.

33

Today my therapist told me that the key to trusting yourself more, to having more tolerance towards stress, and to finding inner emotional stability, is to stop giving a fuck. Fuck what people think. Fuck what society thinks. Just stop giving a fuck.

She said that in her posh British accent. It was the most amazing thing ever. I hope she'll be my therapist for the rest of my life.

39

My dad will never walk me down the aisle. I'll never feel his hand in mine as he hands me to my love at the end of that aisle. We'll never have that Daddy-Daughter dance at the reception. I'm in my forties, I've never been married, and I'm mourning a wedding that will never be. I've never been a big "wedding day" person so I'm surprised at how painful this is. This grief thing is such a harrowing journey of unexpected pain. There is no anticipating how it will show up next.

35

Each of the four times my home phone rang yesterday, my first thought was, "Oh, it's probably Dad calling to check on us in the snowstorm."

Four months and two days later.

I fucking hate this.

36

I was feeling very alone yesterday. It felt like the grief of losing my dad, and the loss of my relationship right afterwards, left me very alone with too much to bear all by myself. My closest friend has been my rock, but you cannot lean on one person all the time, it's not fair to them. I went to sleep last night with my heart feeling very sore and my spirit feeling very small. This morning, two friends each reached out to me, back-to-back, and through them both, I feel a little less alone in my life. I don't write this just to thank them (thank you, Loves!), but to remind people that no matter how strong someone acts, no one is an island. Reach out if you can to someone you care about who is going through a tough time. It's been hard for me because I've always been the one to help hold others together. We all need support, though, especially during the hard times, and that does not make that person weak or incapable. It simply makes them human in all of humanity's wonderful, painful complexity. Don't forget them. Don't leave them alone in the wilderness of their sorrow.

37

There's an inherent insanity to grief that's hard to explain . . . even for a writer.

The pain you feel while grieving brings you so close to the edge of sanity that sometimes you don't know whether to take a step back or hurl yourself off of that cliff into the abyss.

Today feels like a day in which I could leap into it willingly.

38

My kid's teacher at pick-up today: He had a lot of wiggles in his body today but luckily he has even more smarts in his brains.

My kid: Brain. Not brains. You only have one brain.

#DefinitelyMyChild

#iWishDaddyHadBeenThere

#HeDefinitelyWouldveLaughed

#Hard

39

The problem with having been everyone else's "rock" when you find yourself grieving and almost completely depleted of strength, is that others expect you to be there for them the way you always have, and that's just not possible anymore. Talking to friends about being an empath (feeling other people's emotions), I realized that recently I have had to constantly assess if what I'm feeling is my own shit or someone else's. I don't mind carrying someone else's pain for a minute if they need me to lift a heavy boulder while they do the hard work of wriggling out from underneath it, but if you just want me to stand there hoisting this thing up over my head while you lay around and feed yourself grapes, I'm going to have to let this here boulder go.

Especially when I'm over here saving myself all by myself.

I'm not the same Issa anymore. I never will be again.

10

I remembered something today. I'm pretty damn awesome when I'm not being crippled by grief and depression.

I had completely forgotten that.

41

I've been getting vivid flashes of my childhood since my dad's been gone. Movies, songs, smells, emotions. Just now, a sudden, unbearable ball of regret just welled up within my solar plexus because as a teen I threw away my books from when I was a kid, and had I not, right now I would have the *Choose Your Own Adventure: The Mystery of Chimney Rock* book to pass down to my kid, which he would've loved as much as I did. This literally almost brought me to tears. That I have lost not only my father, the epitome of my youth and of my being a "child," but the books that defined my youth as well, made me want to bawl.

This is the insanity of grief.

92

When I once lamented the fact that I was unmarried, my dad said, "As a cop, when someone gets murdered, the first person we look at is the spouse. That should tell you all you need to know about marriage."

Right.

I'm good.

Netflix and sleep it is.

93

What if you operated from the place that where you are right now is where you're supposed to be? That you are not broken? That there isn't something you're supposed to do that you aren't doing? That grieving while muddling through somehow is not only "more than enough," it's all there is to do?

I'm going to try to choose to dwell in that place today.

I hope you can try to as well.

44

I couldn't care less about the supposed romance of this day, I never did, but this is the first Valentine's Day I won't get roses delivered to me by my dad. That's what hurts, I don't care about being single.

This year of "firsts" can already go ahead and kiss my ass and I'm only a few months in.

45

My friend gave me a free ticket to a concert I would love to attend tonight but now I can't go because something came up and I have no child care. This is when I miss my dad like I miss a limb because he would've come right over. I don't know which is worse today, my single mom blues or my fatherless child blues.

96

Oh, hey!

Guess what happens in the new Kung Fu Panda movie!

Po reunites with his dad! Hooray for him that he gets his dad back!

forces self not to throw drink at movie screen

eats more artery-clogging popcorn instead

feels completely insane for being jealous of a cartoon panda

47

When talking to my therapist about my last relationship, she made a reference to a viral video making the internet rounds about a momma cat hugging her kitten who seems to be in the midst of a nightmare. She said that what we all need most, and certainly what I needed most during this hellish past year, was that one person who would hold me close and make me feel safe enough to calm the nightmare that was my life. She insists that just because I have yet to have that doesn't mean I never will. Mostly I don't believe that, if I'm to be completely honest. Yet, sometimes I still hope. A small part of me still can't help it. Maybe one day I will find the love I can stay with for good. Maybe one day there will be someone there to sit beside me during a nightmare and hold me close. Maybe. One day.

48

Tough weekend. I'm starting to think that last year irreparably broke my heart. Between the grief over my dad's loss and then my relationship ending right afterwards, I don't think my heart is going to recover this time. I'm grateful I still have my kid and my mom so that I remember what it feels like to be loved unconditionally.

19

I'm an extremely strong person, but every now and then I need someone to take my hand and tell me that everything will be okay. I don't know if
the fact that the only person who does this anymore is my son is a good thing
or a bad thing. I've busted my ass, especially during the horror this last year
has been, to protect his childhood and to not allow him to be my emotional
caregiver. Children should never be parentified and be made to feel responsible for the well-being of their parent(s). I do want to raise a kind, loving, and
empathetic human being, though, so I often find myself smack in the middle
of how to do so without engendering this kind of hand-holding to a toxic
extent when things have been especially hard for me since my dad passed
away. I wish I didn't always worry that I'm doing this all wrong.

50

"There's no way around grief and loss: You can dodge all you want, but sooner or later you just have to go into it, through it and, hopefully, come out the other side. The world you find there will never be the same as the world you left." — Johnny Cash

51

My therapist told me today that in all her years in this job, she's never met anyone as cognitively and emotionally strong as I am, and that if I ever doubt my ability to persevere that I should look back at the horrors of these last five months (some of which I have not written about publicly), and acknowledge that I got myself through them all. That I'm still getting myself through them. Yes, with help. But it was me in the end that sought the help and fully utilized it. She said I'm an exceptional woman and that while I always find it way too difficult to be proud of myself, that she, and likely others who truly know me and care for me, will be proud of me for me until I can take over. So, of course, that made me bawl.

I'm still bawling.

I miss my Daddy.

52

The only thing that brings me mild momentary relief from the onslaught of grief is that the last thing I said to my dad was, "I love you."

53

My father lives on through my son. My son is a muthafucking gangsta.

Had it been me who was bullied by the staff of my former school for being an atypical learner who needs additional support, I wouldn't have ever wanted to return to that place. I would've avoided it at all cost and wanted nothing more than to put it behind me for once and for all. This school was sued in a class action suit of former parents for the horrible ways they treated their non-neurotypical learners. This school is a nightmare. Had I gone there and experienced the trauma he did, I would never step foot in that place for as long as I lived.

Not my kid.

My son's best friend still goes to his old school. He asked his best friend's mom if he could go with her to pick him up today. I refuse to go back to that school because I'm afraid of going to jail. So, off he went with her to his former Torture School. Once he got there, everyone acted like a superstar alumnus had returned. Everyone who asked how he was, he told that he was doing GREAT. Then, the teacher who made his life miserable rushed to greet him and he graciously hugged her back, and when she asked how he was doing in his new school he told her that the old school, "Wasn't the right fit for me. So I'm doing really great there now. I'm good now. I'm better than I could've ever been in this place." Then he proceeded to walk through the school like he was LeBron James visiting an underprivileged school that he funds, or like a prince waving at all of his subjects, nodding royally at all of the teachers who once tortured him but now feigned excitement to see him, like they were mere peons.

I sat there listening to this story with more delight than I can possibly express.

My father lives on through my son. My son is a muthafucking gangsta.

59

A group text sent to my friends:

Hello, Loves.

May I ask of those who have had to help young children cope with the death of a close relative: What resources have helped you, and what supports have helped you support your grieving babies?

My baby . . . Let's just say he's been missing his Grandpa way more than he was willing to let on to me. He's been protecting his mama. I told him that wasn't his job, he is only eight years old. Now I have to get on with my own job as his parent. My dad was, in a lot of ways, almost like his dad, too. Grandpa was "Big Daddy" around here. T has his own big grief he's been feigning "resilience" around for far too long.

So! What resources helped you and your babies? Please reach out to me individually if this is a conversation you'd prefer to have in private and in confidence — whatever you'd like. I'd be ever so grateful. I really would.

Thank you.

55

I resent grief.

I resent feeling like I'm fine, like just maybe I'm going to be ok, like since I've had a few good days strung together that just maybe I'm on an upward trajectory out of the agony of grief; feeling hope, that false friend, just to have a tsunami of pain wash over me again, leaving me barely able to move.

I resent the good days.

I resent the ways in which good days make you feel as if you are strong and resilient and every bit of the warrior he raised you to be. I resent how it makes you feel as if there could be a light at the end of the tunnel that is not, in fact, an oncoming train. I resent how easily those better days can be dashed against the rocks, shattered, left for rubble. Just like your heart.

I resent the good days, the bad days, and all of the days in between. I resent the way I have been torn apart by something I had no control over, and yet I'm expected to have control over how I move forward from this.

I resent my dad for leaving. I resent him for abandoning me. I resent him for abandoning my kid.

See? Grief makes you insane.

Oh God . . . how I resent this grief.

56

That moment when you tell someone that you just don't know how you will make it through, and they tell you what a source of strength you've been to them, how when they are going through things you always seem to say something that not only speaks to them but encourages and strengthens them, and all you could do was shake your head, thinking, "You don't know. You just don't know how very small and broken I am."

And I am. But at the end of the day, who is stronger than the person who feels they cannot go one step further, not one more, and yet they do. That's all I have. That's all that's left right now. The single step.

"Just one more step, Issa."

Just one more step.

It's going to have to be enough for now.

57

I feel more broken than ever.

Still taking it one step at a time.

I'm still here, though.

I'm still here.

58

When someone sends you an early-morning message saying that they just heard about your dad, and in offering their condolences they write that they have never in all their life ever seen a father love their child as much as he did me. That they have never seen a father as devoted to his child as he was to me. And even though that is supposed to fill you with love and gratitude for him it breaks you wide the fuck open.

My capacity for bearing pain seems never-ending. It's going to take everything I have to get up from this bed today.

59

You know you're dealing with some heavy-ass pain if your steely British therapist starts tearing up and wiping her eyes during your session. I'm so glad that I've got someone showing me just how deeply hard and intense and painful everything I'm going through is. Not that I didn't already know that, but sometimes a little validation goes a long way.

60

That slow realization, after countless therapy sessions, that allows you to understand that you didn't ask for too much, you just asked the wrong person. They were never going to give you the love and support you deserved — even during the profound grief of losing a parent — because they are incapable of it, and it had nothing to do with you. It never did have anything to do with you. They simply didn't have it to give. That says more about them than it could ever say about you, about your "worth," about what you deserve. I'm so glad to have arrived at this understanding.

Therapy is for winners.

61

"Mama, it's Grandpa's fault he died."

"Why would you say that?"

"Because if he hadn't saved those people in the World Trade Center he would still be here with us."

Oh God . . .

My heart . . .

62

A year ago today he went in for a simple overnight procedure and didn't come out of the hospital for over six weeks — ten days of it spent sedated and intubated in the ICU, during which I made every single decision for him as his health care proxy, sleeping in a reclining chair in his room while my mother stayed at my apartment with my son.

He was dead five months later.

I had no idea what was in store for us. It was such a nightmare I still can't believe I made it through. I can't describe the pain of being by his bedside the night they told me he likely wouldn't make it to the next morning and begging him to stay. I looked at his doctor straight in the eyes and told him that they will bring him back as many fucking times as it takes. I fought so damn hard for him. The ICU team wouldn't even do their rounds on him if I wasn't there because they knew I had better be a part of the team's decisions for that day or all hell would break loose. All of my fighting . . . and to only be given five more months with him.

I thought that night was the worst night of my life, the night they told me he likely wouldn't make it and I should call for the chaplain. I had no idea that night would be nothing compared to five months later. I worked so damn HARD to make sure he'd make it. Sometimes I feel like I went through all of that for nothing. For fucking nothing. He still died. He's still gone.

And then I remember that when he first gained consciousness and was extubated, his first words to me were a whispered, "Issa . . . I was going . . . but I'm back now . . . and I want you to know something . . . I love you so fucking much. More than life itself. I always have."

Maybe it wasn't for nothing after all.

63

My kid made me cry today.

I was flustered this morning, doing too much as usual, trying to get everything together to take him to school, and cranky as hell, and he looked up at me and said, "You've been through a lot lately. Let's just take it easy."

He was born with my empath heart. I feel sad for the extra pain he will carry because of it. I feel proud that he will be an agent of love on this planet because of it. Such is the exquisite pain of parenting. Especially while grieving.

69

My kid jumps on top of me as I'm lying on the couch, and I feign death, saying, "Aaaah, I can't breathe! I'm dying!"

He — very seriously — replies, "NO! MAMA, NO! My soul would be crushed if you died!!!"

Yeah, no trauma caused by my dad's death around these parts.

Nope.

None at all.

65

I hate the taste of the word "was" in my mouth when I'm referring to my dad.

66

My mind has been so bogged down with grief that I forgot to pack my son's lunch this morning, so now I feel incredibly inept at life as a whole and I'm absolutely certain my son will remember this and the subsequent school peanut butter and jelly sandwich he'll be forced to eat in the lunchroom as the reason he became a serial killer. The Cult of Motherhood is going to write think pieces about how I'm the reason America is on the decline as a world superpower. He'll tell his children all about how he was neglected and abandoned and that's why he doesn't allow peanut butter or jelly in their home.

Therapy is going great — thanks for asking.

67

I told my therapist that I haven't been doing a good job of juggling all of my responsibilities and I keep dropping balls everywhere. She said I have the most mental and emotional strengths out of all of her clients and that she has full faith in me to do what I need to do to get things done, so naturally my instinct is to find a different therapist because she can't possibly know what she's talking about.

Quack.

This self-love thing is going swimmingly.

68

This is going to be my first birthday without him and I can't adequately express how excruciating it is to not have him here with me.

69

The day he passed away, someone, I can't remember who it was, told me that grief comes in waves. It does, I know that, but I didn't feel it that way then. Grief was crushing me under the constant weight of the house that had collapsed onto my chest, and the idea that this could be fluid, something with variations in intensity, was unimaginable. Grief wasn't waves, grief was the bricks of your own home, the home you lived in for forty-two years, raining down in a hail of tons. You're crushed and bleeding and broken. Ever catching your breath again seems an impossibility. The concept of grief as variable, like waves, like something with an ebb and a flow, seemed very much as if it were a perspective I wasn't physically capable of arriving at.

Somehow I did, though.

You will, too. You will.

Eight months ago today was the last time I saw my dad, but he was already dead when I did see him. Eight months ago today.

Today I'm going out and celebrating making it to another birthday. He would've wanted me to have fun. He would've wanted me to celebrate the life of the kid he loved so very much. So, I'm gonna put on a pretty dress, I'm gonna put some makeup on my face, and I'm gonna "... *pick my Afro, Daddy, 'cuz it's flat on one side.*"

70

When finally getting a long-overdue tombstone for your father's grave triggers a massive depressive episode right when you feel like you're at your strongest and you realize that you will always be a depressive and nothing will ever change that because it is literally encoded into your DNA and your heart breaks for the image you had just so damn recently of a whole Issa that will never be.

71

Me: C'mere, Pun'kin; I want to hug you.

T: Mama, are you sad?

Me: Yes.

T: About Grandpa?

Me: Mostly, yes. But you know what's the one thing that makes me feel better?

T: Me?

Me: Yes. You.

T: You, too, Mama. You always make my day.

I wouldn't be here without this kid. I pray I'm not doing this grief thing badly in front of him.

72

Can't get out of bed today.

Thank God it's a Saturday.

Rock bottom has a cellar.

73

Someone recently asked me what I do for a living and I said, "Nothing. I am living off of my savings while I am in recovery from a major depressive episode triggered by the grief of my father's passing." She immediately said, "I'd like to congratulate you. Congratulations on making your recovery a priority."

A decade ago, I would've been looked at as a lazy piece of garbage, a loser, a nothing. In this country, more so than in many others, who you are is based on what you "do." Who am I if I'm not "doing" anything? I mean, I can always say that I'm a stay at home mom, which I am, but that never seems to be "enough," especially when you had a vibrant career in which you no longer engage. You always have to be a stay at home mom AND a volunteer, AND a blogger, AND a soccer team coach. We are not allowed to be a human being, we have to be a human *doing*. The worst is that saying, "Writers write," as if when you cease to write, you are no longer a writer. Writing is in my blood, my brain, my soul. I'll never not be a writer. Except, I haven't been able to write anything substantial in a while. So, lately I've been a huge underachiever. A nothing. A loser. Those are the words that my broken brain uses against me on the bad days. Those are the thoughts that what's left of the *real me* rails against. Those are some of the ways in which I struggle to regain a more holistic sense of self.

But this past Saturday, someone congratulated me on choosing to do nothing but focus on my recovery. And for the briefest of moments, I wasn't a loser. A nothing. A has-been. I was a survivor. A fighter. A force to be reckoned with. For the briefest of moments, I could let go of the shame that lays in bed with me on the nights when no matter how many times I turn my pillow over, it never seems cool enough against my face.

This is what mental health awareness looks like in this day and age — a "Congratulations." The shame and the stigma that comes with a mental illness diagnosis is slowly being disintegrated due to the brave voices that speak up and out against it. I have done this work for many years now, both online and off, but now, when my father's passing has left me with only my son who truly needs me, I need the shame to be eradicated more than ever.

I fight for my well-being for my son even more than I fight for myself. He saves me. He helps me to save myself. I look forward to the day when my well-being matters because I matter as Issa, not just as his mom.

There is still an enormous amount of work to be done to eliminate the stigma and shame surrounding struggling with mental well-being, especially in communities of color. With every voice that speaks up to share their stories, either publicly or one-on-one, we get closer to the day that getting a mental illness diagnosis like depression, anxiety, or Complex PTSD, is no more shame-filled than getting an arthritis diagnosis. I will keep speaking up, I will keep using my voice to stand up for those in the mental health community, and I will keep working toward the day that the shame that far too often accompanies mental health struggles will be a thing of the past.

There is no shame in mental illness, or in working toward mental health. How could there be? Since when is someone ashamed of a warrior?

79

Today my therapist looked me in the eyes and said, "I'm afraid of how you sound. You sound like you've completely given up on yourself, on any chance of having a happy life. I have sixty – and seventy-year old clients who look back and most regret that they gave up on themselves and their chances of ever being happy. Of having loving relationships. Of achieving difficult personal goals. They look back and feel like it's too late to get any of the things they hoped they'd get out of life. You're in your early forties and you sound just like them. Please don't give up on yourself. Please don't just keep living for your son only. You deserve to be happy. You deserve to be loved as well."

Damn.

75

My Kid: Mama, you know how we talked about that Grandpa is a spirit and watches us now?

Me: Yes, Baby?

Him: That creeps me out.

Me, surprised, cracking up: Well, I don't think he's in every room with us all of the time staring at us. I think he's just out there as an energy that helps protect us.

Him: What could he do to protect us? Ghosts can't touch stuff.

Me: I think that when you get the feeling inside of something being dangerous, or that you should stay away from a person or a place, that's Grandpa helping you to protect yourself from something bad.

Him: Ohhh, ok. I get it now.

This kid. I'm still laughing.

76

Trying to remember something and I couldn't. I then think, "Maybe I should ask Dad if he remembers."

Fuck you, Brain.

Asshole.

77

I've noticed since my father passed that my kid leaves the room if I cry. He doesn't want to see me in pain and just leaves. I'm trying to figure out how to get him to stop doing that because when he grows up and his partner is hurting, I don't want him to abandon them during their times of pain. I'm trying to figure out the healthiest way to do this, though, because I don't want to force my pain onto him. I need to research ideas on how to go about this process in the healthiest way possible.

78

Bizarre dream last night.

I was in a long hallway, I think I was in a school. I saw my dad, in his police uniform, who was giving treats to kids. At first I didn't believe it was him, and I walked over to him. I asked if it was really him and he said yes, and then I touched him for good measure to be sure he was corporeal. Once I realized he was real I lost it. He went to hold me and I started crying and screaming and had to be tranquilized, but then next thing I knew I was in my own room at home. My mom was there taking care of my kid, and my closest friends were also there. They asked me if I was okay, and asked me what my plans were to "get better." I then proceed to violently curse every single one of them out: my mother, my closest friends, the few people who have actually been there for me throughout this mess. The few people I'm grateful for. Cursed them ALL the way out, violently. Then I threw everyone out of my room and proceeded to rearrange the furniture in my room and throw tons of stuff out. I had just moved in and mended a kid's slightly broken bed next to my queen-sized bed (we live in a two-bedroom apartment, my kid has his own room, and it wasn't his bed), and then I brought out the stuff I was throwing away into my apartment's hallway. Everyone asked me again if I was okay and I proceeded to tell them the hell off again.

"I CAN'T BE WHAT YOU WANT ME TO BE!!! I CANNOT HEAL THE WAY YOU WANT ME TO!!! I CAN'T BE 'OKAY' FOR YOUR GOTDAMN COMFORT!!!"

Then I woke up.

The anniversary of my father's passing is next month. You'd think almost a year later I wouldn't still be doing this.

79

Holding out hope that the light at the end of the tunnel isn't an oncoming train.

80

I just did something with my hand that my father always did, and my heart feels like someone reached in and pulled out an artery. The ways in which he lives on in me should comfort me, and sometimes they do. Other times, though, they serve only to remind me that he is dead.

My father is dead.

Those words, eleven months later, still make me hurt in a way that renders me paralyzed, as if the shock is just too large for my system to bear.

81

In the last two days, two of my dearest friends, knowing my kid was at my mother's house in Pennsylvania, came over with wine and friendship. They listened and talked and were just "there."

When you know someone is going through their own personal "Dark Times" but you don't know what to do? Go over with a bottle (or two) of wine. Or tea or coffee, if they don't drink. Sit with them and remind them that they matter to you. I assure you, that simple gesture will make all the difference in the world to their tired, battered hearts.

82

Where the fuck is Calgon?

Why won't it take me away?

83

I told someone that I rent my apartment, and that the only land I own happens to have my father's body in it, and then laughed at my own dark joke.

The look of horror on their face . . . It was beyond priceless.

I have clearly come to the part of grieving in which I make horribly inappropriate jokes in a fruitless attempt to ameliorate the emotional waterboarding that is losing a loved one. How fun.

(My dad would've found these jokes hilarious, by the way. Morbid humor for the win.)

89

I think someone should tell you that after the first year of loss, the year of grief to which all manner of successes and failures are attributed to and excused by, a sense of peace doesn't always come. I think you should know that when the year has passed, some of you will feel more pain than you did at the outset. The numbness is finally gone and now you can fully feel the true brokenness of your heart. The holidays, as we all already know, can have a way of crushing a sharpness to the edges of those broken pieces. For some, the pain of healing has only just begun now that the year of firsts has gone by and the necessary numbness to deal with all of that pain has worn away. You are not in the home stretch, no. It is deeply frustrating to have to accept that. Maybe the "home stretch" for profound grief takes its own meandering amount of time. Just know that I get it. That a year later you were expecting some measure of transcendence and all you got was the anesthesia during an amputation turned all the way down. I understand you completely. I do.

Please hang in there. You've made it this far. You will make it even further. You will. I promise.

85

Sometimes it gets hard to be brave enough to face all the pain life can bring.

I still don't know how I do it. I really don't.

To whomever is carrying a weight in their heart that feels unbearable — please, hang in there. Those of us who haven't hardened our hearts to this brutal life are some of the strongest and bravest around. Hang in there. The beauty shines through eventually, giving us the push to keep going. The rays of light break through into the depths of the murkiest mourning waters, shining the way to the surface.

Hang in there, okay?

I love you.

86

Just picked up my phone to wish my daddy a Merry Christmas.

Over a year later.

The "phantom limb" pain of grief is very real. If you're going through it yourself today, just know you're not alone. I'm in the darkness with you. That arm you feel around your shoulders is mine. I'll sit with you for a while. You're not alone.

87

I still cannot believe he is gone.

knocks bookshelf over

shoves laptop to the floor

flips table

leaves room

slams door

88

Just walked into Starbucks and they're playing The Manhattans' *"Shining Star."* I can hear his voice singing along perfectly in my head, clear as day, just like he used to in our living room when I was a kid. I stood in line and sang along softly while crying. Eighteen months later and I'm still having these moments. Good thing I'm on my way to therapy, I guess.

89

My therapist says that despite what my brain tells me, I'm doing an amazing job considering everything I've been through, and that I am far stronger and more resilient than I even realize. She says I should be proud of myself and how far I've come, not ashamed for not being where I wish I could be.

She's obviously unqualified and has no idea what she's talking about.

Quack.

(Therapy is *clearly* working for me — thanks for asking.)

90

Monday is already Mondaying.

I had a dream I can't quite recall but I know my dad was in it. I woke up singing, *"Heaven Must Be Missing An Angel"* by Tavares, and I could practically hear his voice singing it like when I was little. I used to have that song on 45 vinyl.

Sometimes I wish grief were a person so I could punch it right in the face.

Have a good Monday, though. Seriously. Hope your Monday is great.

Okay, bye.

91

My kid looked at me this morning and said, "I know you still miss Grandpa, Mama. Sometimes I miss him, too. But sometimes I get angry at him. I don't ever want to be a hero. I'm not going to die so strangers can live. I'm gonna be something safe like a video game inventor. The only thing I'm gonna save is my own butt from killer cyborg dinosaurs."

This kid. Tears and laughter, all before 8 am.

92

Sometimes when I think of him I feel like I am the luckiest little girl in the world to have had a daddy who always made me feel like I was loved and cared for, and in those moments it feels like maybe the inner child in me is healing. I think maybe that's how it happens. I think that instead of healing from your mind down, you actually heal from your heart out. Thinking and analyzing and processing is extremely helpful, but in the end, I think it's the child's heart within that leads the way to healing. It's where resilience and forgiveness and love live eternally. It's where anything is possible.

93

April 23.

Happy birthday, Daddy.

I wish you were here.

I love you.

99

Guess what I did today, on my father's birthday, that is making me bawl my eyes out?

My dad could sing. No, my daddy could *saaang*. I grew up with him singing everything from the Stylistics and The Delfonics to Hector Lavoe. I used to love to hear him sing. When I was little, he got an audition to be one of Luther Vandross' background singers, right before Luther first made his debut solo album, but he didn't get the gig. That, among other things, made him buy into the whole "starving artist" idea that you'd never really make it as an artist, so it was better to get a "real" job. So, he stayed a cop instead.

Fast forward, I am fourteen years old. I am leaving the house with my mother to go to my singing audition at LaGuardia High School (the "Fame" school, for non-New Yorkers). My dad looks at me and says, not "good luck," or "break a leg," but, "I don't know why you're bothering. Even if you get in I'm not letting you go there. You're way too smart to waste your life struggling; you're going to a regular academic high school."

And just like that, it was gone. He snatched my dream from me right then and there. The dream I'd had since I was a toddler, holding pencils like microphones and singing into the eraser. I went on the audition anyway, but sang very half-heartedly and didn't get selected, unsurprisingly.

In my early twenties I did some background vocals for a few artists. I did some background vocals once for my then-best friend who is a huge House music artist. I sang with friends and I sang in the shower, but I never again saw myself as a "singer," not really.

I know my dad "meant well"; he didn't want me to live a life of struggle and disappointment. This is a prime example, however, of why people's best intentions do not absolve them of the impact of their actions.

Back to today. Today, I reached out to a friend who is also a vocal coach within the Broadway community. I am going for vocal coaching. I am going to sing again. It's been far too long. I'm going to do this for me, not for a role or a record deal, but to remind myself that it's never too late to pick an old dream back up. To remind myself that the sins of the father can be laid to rest with him. To remind myself to truly live while I'm still alive.

95

Me: I'm doing the Whole30 diet right now. My last day will be two days before my birthday so I can go out and have some drinks and enjoy myself.

My therapist: Gin has no carbs.

Me: See, and this is exactly why you've been the best therapist I've ever had.

96

Some people don't want you to heal, because if you do, they know you will grow right past them and let them go. Pay attention to the people who negatively remark upon how "you've changed" when you start to grow and heal. Pay attention to the ways you keep yourself small to keep those people in your life. Pay attention to the way you break yourself off into small, bite-sized chunks to be less of a threat to others. Heal. Make yourself whole again. Become too big to consume, so that when others try to swallow you whole, they choke.

Let 'em choke.

97

Overheard at school drop-off this morning:

Friend: How come you got a dog?

My kid: Because dogs are the best at healing your heart when you've lost someone you love.

98

I just realized that my father's strength, his fierceness, always made me feel safe in the world, no matter where I was, and the last year and a half I've been consumed by fear because I don't know how to be brave and strong and fierce in a world where he doesn't exist.

99

That moment when you're going through a pile of papers and you come across your father's Health Care Proxy form written in his hand designating you as his proxy and you break down and sob.

100

When every time you hear what this Sunday is and you immediately spit out, "Fuck Father's Day," you realize that maybe, just maybe, you're nowhere near healed yet.

101

I'm on a solo vacation in Savannah, GA. And Daddy is always with me. Always protecting me. Always.

I was sitting in front of Forsyth Cafe, sipping my sweet tea, when a panhandler asked me for money. Anyone who knows me knows I always give. Always. But something about this man's energy frightened me, and I didn't want to open my wallet, so I said, "No, I'm sorry." He stood there for a minute, scowling angrily at me, and then walked away to my right. I went back to people watching until I realized he was now sitting at a table to my left, glaring at me. I got up and walked away and looked over my shoulder, and sure enough, he had turned around to watch me leave. I kept waking, turning around immediately to see if he was following, which he wasn't. I walked about 50 – 60 feet away and stopped at a bench off the main fountain area to plug in my phone into an external battery, and when I picked my bag up from the bench I realized he's about ten feet away from me. As I see him, though, who do I see right behind him? Two cops. I have to walk past him to get to the cops, so I do. I walk right towards him and stare at him like he will die if he touches me. Then I walked over to the cops and told them what happened. They told me to go on and they would take care of him, and as I looked back, they were talking to him. I've lived my whole life in New York City and have traveled alone the world over, but that was the most scared I've ever been. He meant to do more than just take my money — he meant to hurt me. I could feel it.

I swear to you on all that I love, that was my daddy bringing those cops to me out of nowhere. I was fine until I got out of the park and to the nearest corner and said out loud, "Thank you, Daddy." I didn't even finish the word "you" before I fell apart. I'm standing here sobbing just thinking about him reaching out his spiritual hand to protect his baby. I'm okay; I'm safe. No way I'm gonna let this get to me and ruin my trip. I don't care what anyone says, though, that was all my Daddy.

What a lucky girl I am.

102

I was trying to enjoy a facial at a spa today and when I laid back and clasped my hands over my chest I immediately yanked them apart — I always do now — because it reminds me of how his hands were resting one over the other on his chest as he lay there dead, and then I started remembering the sound of my screams . . .

Suffice it to say, I didn't get to thoroughly enjoy my facial. Hard to do so with tears pouring into your ears, ya know? It'll be two years this September and it's only gotten marginally easier to carry.

If you're grieving, be gentle with yourself. This process takes so much longer than the "allotted time" of one pathetic year for some of us. Don't let anyone rush you through your own personal process. You get to take as much time as you need and don't believe anyone who tells you any different.

103

Sometimes I want to shout at the world, "Would you get pissed at someone who had his legs amputated for not being able to play sports with you anymore?"

No. No, you would not.

Think about that the next time you shame a person dealing with severe grief, depression, anxiety, or any other mental health issue for not being "a good friend" and maintaining contact. Sometimes reaching out is impossible for someone who is suffering, for reasons you are lucky enough not to understand. If you really love your friend, instead of criticizing them, maybe just keep reaching out to them, let them know you're still there, and that no matter what, you'll be there without anything shitty to say when they *are* able to pick up the phone again. If you're busy focusing on it being "one-sided," you're not understanding the prison your friend is in. Try compassion instead of judgement for that person you claim to love.

109

The best present I ever gave my dad was Jerry Lewis.

In the early 90s, *Damn Yankees*, one of my dad's favorite movies, came to Broadway as a play. The play cast Jerry Lewis as the Devil. Now, my dad LOVED Jerry Lewis. I had grown up watching every single Jerry Lewis movie that ever existed, with my dad making commentary throughout the movies as usual. He had grown up watching those movies as well, and loved them very much. Well, here was my chance to have Daddy see him live, and I wasn't going to miss that opportunity for anything in the world.

The day of my dad's birthday that year fell on a Saturday, and we always spent Saturdays together anyway, so the surprise was going well so far. We met for a late breakfast as usual, before our day of shopping, movies, and walking around the Village took its usual place in our Saturday lives. I told him we had to stay in Midtown because I had a surprise for him. Now, this was a risky move because Daddy hated surprises, I mean absolutely hated them, and I knew it was possible that he would either bail, or make me tell him what it was. As expected, he reminded me that he hated surprises, but I assured him that he would absolutely love this one, and though he remained unconvinced, he grumbled and complained but went along with it. As we were walking to the theater, I pointed at the marquis and said, "Look — Jerry Lewis is in *Damn Yankees*." He nodded his head and replied, "I know," to which I replied, "Happy Birthday, Daddy!" The look of delight on his face is one I will never forget. My dad didn't get many happy moments in his life, and I had just given him one. I was about to give him two hours worth of happiness. We walked into the theater and his excitement was palpable. It was literally like a kid walking into an amusement park. During the intermission he couldn't stop talking about the play, about Jerry, about everything. When the play was over and we walked out, my middle-aged father was a kid again. He seemed to regress in age, his speech bubbly and lyrical. We walked down New York City streets singing, *"Whatever Lola Wants"* and recapping the play a dozen times over. He was the happiest kid on the block. He turned to me and said, "That was the best surprise I've ever had."

Thank you for helping me give my dad a truly happy day, Jerry. He didn't get many of those. Thank you for giving me something good to give my dad on a birthday so long ago. You gave us more than you could ever have known. I wish you peace now that you have gone, I wish you eternal love and laughter, and I wish you all the cigarettes and martinis you could ever want.

Goodbye, Jerry, and thanks for all the laughs.

105

I told my therapist today that the ten days between 9/11 and 9/21 (the day of my father's death), find me just barely coping. She told me to do the barest of minimums until the end of the month. If everyone is fed and the dog is walked, don't do shit else. Close shop and tend to my needs, even if that means doing absolutely nothing. So, that's what I'm gonna do. I'm going to give myself permission to do as much "nothing" as I can, even when I beat myself up for not being productive. Especially then.

Doctor's orders.

106

On September 21st, it'll be two years since he's been gone from life itself. I'm less than. Diminished. Smaller. Irreparably damaged. I am the prisoner of war, kept in an underground cell, broken and hunched, eyes grown almost blind from lack of light.

I am also greater. Stronger. Larger than the ways I had previously shrunk myself. Irrepressibly evolving. I am the prisoner of war, emerging from that cell, still healing but straighter, eyes squinting against a light that hadn't been seen in such a long while.

I send my love to anyone struggling today, or to anyone who has been struggling for a while and feels as if the onslaught will never end and they can't bear another day. I get it. With 9/11 only four days ago and his death day of 9/21 coming next week, I am struggling to retain the dwindling amount of fucks I have left. So, believe me, I feel you. People can be so selfish and cruel and it gets hard to bear life sometimes. I totally get it. All I'm saying is, let's just get through today. We can do this. Just get through today.

We can get through tomorrow together when it gets here.

107

Two years ago today.

I thought I'd be "okay" today but of course I'm writing this through endless tears. In two hours from now, I was told he was gone, and a guttural howl flowed from the opening in my soul that was left by him being ripped away from me. I haven't been the same since. The only thing that saves me is that the last thing I said to him was, "I love you." The cost of love is grief. I know I pay such a steep price because I was so profoundly loved by him, even if it was a flawed, complicated love.

I know I haven't exactly made you "proud" these last two years, Old Man, but I'm getting there. Slowly. The world is a scarier place with you gone, Daddy. In so many ways. I'm sure Theo makes you proud daily and you miss him terribly. He misses you, too. We both do. Please keep watch over us and protect us from anyone who would seek to hurt Theo or me in any way. Help me turn these tears into comfort . . . somehow.

I love you.

108

I pressed "listen" to an unlabeled voice note in my iPhone and heard my father's voice for the first time in two years. I sat there for about thirty seconds before I could fully process what was happening, and then quickly turned it off.

Now I want to stab myself in the head.

How's your day going so far? Better than mine, I hope!

109

Remembering the night that the ICU team came in and told me if he codes they don't think I should try and bring him back. A part of me died at that moment. That night they told me it was time to get the chaplain, and I looked at his doctor straight in the eyes and told him that I wasn't giving up on my father and that they will bring him back as many fucking times as it took. And they did. I fought so hard for him for weeks on end and I thought that I'd pulled him through. His medical team wouldn't even do their rounds on him if I wasn't there and would wait until I arrived if I hadn't spent the night because they knew I had better be a part of his team's decisions for that day or there would be a serious problem they most certainly did not want to deal with.

All of my fighting, all of my advocating, all of that courage . . . and to only be given five more months with him.

I hope I didn't fail him.

Sometimes it still feels like I did.

110

I was going through a pile of old greeting cards and found the last two my dad gave me — Christmas 2014 and my birthday 2015. My birthday was five days after he went home from the hospital. He'd been hearing about what I did while he was intubated and sedated and for days every time I entered his room he would look at me in amazement and tell me another story one of the ICU team members told him about me. About how hard I fought for him. About how I researched anything and everything I possibly could pertaining to his care so that I would be an educated advocate for him. How much they grew to love me. He heard it all.

He wrote the following in that last birthday card:

"You amazed me, and have made me so proud of who you are. I can only say thank you, and I love you more and more each day. To know one's child is a very special thing. But to see how she's grown, and how beautiful and intelligent and capable she's become, what a treasure God has given me in you."

I can barely breathe, I'm crying so hard.

111

That feeling when you've accomplished something, even if it was a small accomplishment, and your father isn't here anymore to be proud of you. It takes a bit of the joy out of it, to be honest. I feel like any accomplishment from here on out will be terribly bittersweet. The heartbreak of grief eventually turns into a small, dull throb — a faint heartache — but it never, ever goes away.

112

I read a piece today about a woman dealing with her mother's terminal illness, and how difficult it was to hold space for the fact that she was dying and wanting to be kind and compassionate with her, while simultaneously acknowledging their difficult history and the ways she felt triggered by the things her mother continued to say to her.

This made me remember all of the many times I lost my patience with my dad and it hurt so deeply that my gut reaction was, "Ohdeargod, how I wish I could do it all over again. I wouldn't have fought with him all those times if I knew I was going to lose him in only a few month's time. Why the fuck did I continue to argue with him, knowing how sick he was? My God . . . how I wish I could do it all over again."

Except, not really. Because losing him a second time would kill me for sure.

113

I miss him so much sometimes it gets hard to breathe. I feel so all alone in this world without him. As I lie in this bed, sick, unable to provide a Thanksgiving holiday for my son, having no choice yesterday but to get up and transport him to and from school while dizzy and aching, walking the dog, providing meals and semi-conscious check-ins on my kid, I have never been more acutely aware of how alone I am in a world where my dad no longer exists.

If you have someone in this world who puts you first in all things, please, *PLEASE*, cherish them. Even if they drive you batshit fucking crazy sometimes like my dad definitely did, let them know how much you appreciate all they have done for you. Let them know how thankful you are today and every day for all they did and all they continue to do. Take a moment today to let them know they mean the world to you. That's the true expression of thanksgiving. Count your blessings in love today, if you can. You can't begin to truly understand their value in your life until they are no longer here.

119

I am my father's child in too many ways to count. It is terrifying.

115

I never saw myself as a "Dog Person." I had a cat for fifteen years and when she died in 2009 I didn't think I could bear the loss of another animal, so I decided I wouldn't have them again.

Then, as you know, my kid and I lost my dad in September of 2015. My kid then spent the following year lobbying for a dog, and I flat-out refused. Over and over and over again. But at some point around the end of November 2016, I started getting the thought in my head that maybe a dog could help him with the difficulties he was going through. I didn't even think of myself because I didn't see how a dog could ever begin to fill the hole in my heart, but my kid's therapist confirmed that having an emotional support animal would work wonders for him, so I did what I always do for him — anything I possibly can.

A year ago today we "fostered" Jake for a weekend to see if we (read: I), could actually take this on. He never left. And while no one could ever fill the hole in my heart left by my father's absence, this little trouble maker has been quite the balm. We love him so very much and cannot fathom life without him. My kid said just today, "You know what I love about dogs, Mom?"

"No, what?"

"They help your heart heal when it's broken."

He's right. They really do.

116

That moment when you're in a Starbucks, and are in the middle of speaking a sentence, and you abruptly stop mid-word and start uncontrollably crying because a song suddenly comes on that your father loved and you can hear your daddy singing along with it just like he used to when you were a kid. This happens to me so often that you would think I'd be used to it by now, but alas, there is no getting used to this kind of pain.

117

Sometimes I'll make a face and I can feel that it's a face my father used to make and that realization both makes me smile and breaks my heart all at once.

118

I often talk about how alike my dad and I were. There were many ways in which we couldn't have been more different from each other, though. I just watched a video about people who are placing their remains into biodegradable urns filled with their ashes that you can plant a tree seed into. The deceased then grows into a tree.

When I die I would want my kid to do this for me.

If I had done this to my dad, however, he would've come back from the grave, woken my ass up from a deep sleep, and yelled right in my face, "You turned me into a fucken tree???"

I'm laughing so hard just thinking of it.

119

My father's overwhelming love and devotion to me was both blessing
and burden. If you've never been a parent's "everything," that's hard to understand. But, and I'm crying as I write this now, as much as that man was the
center of my whole life, there is a devastating sort of freedom when a parent
like that passes. On one hand, you are now incomplete — missing a limb,
missing your core. On the other hand, you are now free to be completely
yourself in the way that only losing a parent can make you. There are no more
moments of, "I can't do that; Daddy would be so disappointed." Now there
is only, "Where have I hidden who I truly am? How do I go about expressing
that in a way that feels less like killing my father and more like giving birth
to myself?"

Two years later and I'm still figuring that out.

120

Do you believe that loved ones can send you messages from the other side via music?

I kept telling myself they were all little coincidences, but over the last six months in particular I keep getting sent such highly specific songs that I can't ignore it anymore.

My dad has been coming to me a lot lately.

I just happened to "randomly" come across a video of Sydney Poitier singing in one of his old films, and I was ten years old again, and my daddy and I are watching "Lilies of the Field" together on a late Sunday afternoon, and we are singing the song *"Amen"* together as if he were Sydney and I were one of the nuns, and he is still the healthiest, strongest man in the world, and I was loved and I was protected, and the world was safe and still so very good.

121

Elderly upstairs neighbor: Oh, hi! Hey, how's your father? I haven't seen him in a long time.

Me: . . . deep fucking sigh . . .

122

I just saw an old clip of Danny Kaye performing live and I teared up. I wish I could show it to my dad. I grew up watching all of Danny Kaye's movies with him, usually on lazy Sunday afternoons. We loved Danny Kaye.

Hey Daddy, wherever you are, don't forget "a pint of Prospect Park."

123

I just bought tickets to our first play since my dad died. That was our thing. My dad and I saw at least two Broadway shows a year. When I clicked "Purchase Tickets" I felt a knot in my solar plexus and my throat began to close. Tears filled my eyes when the purchase was confirmed.

It's been two years and five months.

And still.

IT'S SO FUCKING HARD! I DON'T WANT TO DO THIS SHIT WITHOUT HIM! ANY OF IT!!!

But he would've wanted his grandchild to see Broadway shows, for him to love them as much as we did. So, I do it for his grandson. He would've wanted *me* to live a good life too, though, because he worked his ass off to make sure I had a good life while he was here. So, I'm going. It's just that he would've wanted to be right there with us at the play. That's the hardest part. Going without him. Going on without him. It's always the hardest part of everything.

124

When people discuss their fears or pain or grief, and are told they are "being negative" or "focusing on the bad" and that they should "be more positive," it makes me so unbelievably angry. Nobody needs that kind of gaslighting. The Cult of Positivity has made it a moral failing to do what is absolutely necessary: Identify your fears and/or pain, discuss them with someone you trust, and then construct a plan of action. These days the second you open your mouth to identify your fears or your sadness you're labeled as "focusing on the negative," and if you're the kind of person who has to process things for a while before you take action, well then you're just "wallowing."

That, my friends, is bullshit.

You have every right to identify and discuss your fears, your pain, your grief. You have every right to feel sad, angry, disappointed, or worried. *ALL* of your feelings in the face of an upsetting situation are valid. Should you just complain all the time and not eventually take action? Of course not. Take action, always, but do it when *you* are ready. Don't let anyone tell you how long to take in order to process things. Don't let anyone try to slap you with a, "Just make a gratitude list and stop focusing on negativity!" Fuck that noise. Take as long as you need to process before you take the action you think is best. And if anyone tells you that you're being negative while you do so, tell them that you're positive — that they're an asshole.

125

Sometimes grief looks like trying to get ready to take your kid out to see Aladdin on Broadway tonight for his half-birthday, but you've been crabby and weepy all day about stepping into a theatre without the old man, and what you really want to do is cancel and climb into bed for the rest of the night.

126

At one point in the play there's a scene where Pearl sings to her father, "Daddy, can you hear me?" and my kid reached over and put his hand on my back.

This kid.

I thank everything in the universe for him.

127

It's interesting to me that so many people say, "I'm sorry," when they cry. Looking forward to the day that crying isn't seen as a weakness we need to apologize for.

128

It just dawned on me that my dad won't be there to watch my kid graduate from elementary school. My stomach hurts.

129

A man walked past me who smelled exactly like my dad. In mere nano-seconds I went from wanting to punch him in the face to wanting to hug him and never let go.

130

I read an article by a medical professional that talked about how far too many families put their dying relatives on breathing machines and that, usually, it's not in the best interest of the patient. Reading that made me realize that it's one of the only things that brings me a modicum of peace when I think of how my dad chose to leave. And I do believe his spirit chose to leave. They put him on a home oxygen machine and exactly a week later he was gone. His heart literally ruptured in his chest. He refused to live out the rest of his life as anything but the incredibly strong superhero that he was, and while I'll never get over his loss, sometimes, underneath all the pain, I understand.

I do.

131

If you are recently bereaved, you probably feel like you are coming apart at the seams. I know. And sadly, all I can say is that there is nothing nor anyone that will bring you out of it, except for the passage of time. Not to say that you will ever stop grieving. You won't. Yet the pain gets less intense, more bearable, and joy sneaks back into your life in small ways at first — and then more so over time — and at some point you realize you're listening to a song he loved and instead of wishing the ground would open up and swallow you whole, you smile and nod your head and say, "How lucky I was, even if I had to lose him. How lucky I was to have had him at all."

You don't think that day will ever come, but somehow it does, and you realize you've come through the worst of it, certainly worse for the wear, but also deeply confident in your ability to weather what life brings you because you lived through such abject grief.

If you are newly bereaved, I send you love and compassion today and every day. Be extra kind to yourself. You deserve it.

132

The fact that I was able to get through yesterday, the third anniversary of his death, without unbearable amounts of grief and pain is extraordinary to me. I broke down once in the late morning hours after my kid was at school and I had run some errands, and I was home alone with nothing but my thoughts and my misshapen heart. I broke down and I cried . . . I told my dad that I missed him, and I thanked him for loving me so much that I am still supported by his love and guidance, and I cried loud, guttural sobs that pulled from my diaphragm and rasped my throat. And then, I just . . . . stopped. Almost as suddenly as I'd begun to cry, I was done. It was over. The intensity of the pain was gone and I could start drying my face with the Starbucks napkin wrapped around my cold brew. I was done. I could move on from this. Indeed, I was doing just that.

Was it a defense mechanism to keep me from sliding down the slippery slope of complex grief into the hell of depression? Or am I stronger now after three years without him than I ever thought I'd be? Both, probably. Probably a lot of both. The important part is that I was kinda sorta scared of "THE THIRD ANNIVERSARY!" and yet, somehow, I muddled through. Look at me growing n' shit. It's almost like I'm an amazing human being or something.

I want to thank everyone who texted/called/Facebook messaged/smoke signaled me love yesterday, on the third anniversary of my hero of a father dying. In many ways I'm far worse for the wear of these past three years, but in the ways that most matter I've grown beyond measure, and your love and friendships have been a part of what's supported me while in the process of healing. Thank you for loving Issa when I couldn't love her, when all she could do was pour what love she had left in a world of grief into the grandson her father loved so very much. Thank you for all of the many ways you've been there for my kid and me. The people in my village are some of the best people in the whole entire world.

133

My therapist told me today that I needed to give myself full and unconditional consent to do the bare minimum when I feel run down by responsibility, grief, or any other heavy thing. That I need to give myself permission to do only the things that come from an internal place of desire as opposed to external expectations placed upon me, and to actively choose things that bring me personal pleasure and joy. That doing less isn't being irresponsible, it's the very definition of self-care.

I thought you might need this message today as well.

139

Watching a video in which a mom surreptitiously records her son as he grooves to an oldies song, and it reminds me of a moment with my dad. I was around 6 or 7 years old, and the song *"One In A Million"* by Larry Graham was out. My parents and I were on their bed listening to music, and that song came on the radio. I closed my eyes, sang my heart out, and when the song was over and I opened my eyes, my parents were sitting there, mouths agape, in total silence. Then they both started clapping and cheering like crazy. I'll never, ever forget that moment for as long as I live.

Aaaand now I'm crying. Ugh.

135

As Christmas approaches, I'd like to take a moment to acknowledge that this year has brought such tremendous growth to me in my life that I went from someone who, for three interminable years, was a zombie — only continuing to "live" for my son — to someone who feels embodied and alive for the first time in over three years. I feel closer to the real me than I've felt in ages. And you know what? *I* did that. I saved myself. Yes, my therapist, my mom, my best friend, and the people in my village helped me, but at the end of it all, it was me who got strong enough to pull myself out of the abyss. And, my God, what an abyss it was. It was so fucking dark in there. I was so scared and alone. I didn't think I'd ever find my way back. Some days got so bad I'd resent my kid for forcing me to continue to live. I didn't know if I'd ever stop feeling like I had no skin, or like I was walking on broken legs, I just knew I had to keep going for the sake of my son. Anything for him. And like a beacon toward safety, I just followed the light of my love for him, and at some point I looked up and I wasn't limping anymore. I haven't limped in months. I still get anxiety because my brain is a lovable asshole sometimes. I get tired, and far too maudlin, and I still cry at the drop of a hat when others are hurting because being an empath is like that sometimes. But I don't limp anymore. I walk strong and sure and I breathe fire only when someone deserves it. Sometimes not even then. No one deserves my peace. Sometimes the worst thing you can do to someone is remove the glory of your loving energy from them. No fuss. Just a smile and a wave and a, "Fare thee well." There's no need for the fight when you feel strong. My strength feels like an old friend returning from too long of an absence. My strength feels like armor I don't even need anymore.

I'm writing this to say, the holidays can be so damn hard, I know, and if you were already struggling with emotional pain before the holidays hit, that pain just tends to get harder to bear during this upcoming week. Please believe me when I tell you, I absolutely understand that. I know that pain and how you will do anything to *make.it.stop.* I know that some days it feels like it will never stop, but you can't believe your brain when it tells you that because sometimes grief and depression are liars who will do anything to get you to stay in your abusive relationship with it.

Don't let your pain gaslight you into thinking that you and your loved ones would be better off without you here. That's utter bullshit.

And while I'm not going to give you empty platitudes about "it gets better" (because how the fuck do I know if it actually gets better? Tomorrow may come and find me curled up in the fetal position once again for all I know), and while grief doesn't ever go away, it merely chills the fuck out for small periods of time, I can tell you there will be days when you'll feel almost whole again — and that glimpse of your real self will release the vise grip that grief and depression have around your heart. Like someone dealing with a chronic physical illness, just do what you can when you are well, so that when you are once again unwell, you can rest and gather strength for your next remission. The resting part is crucial: use the next week to go as easy on yourself as you can. And if you can't yet see that glimpse of your real self, reach out to a loved one and ask them to remind you of who you really are. Your bound heart will swell against its restraints upon hearing itself recognized.

Please, hold on. To a loved one. To the promise of a better day. To the inevitability of a stronger you. If you can't fight right now, don't. Just hold on. Wrap your arms around the possibility of feeling expansive and free and don't let go until the waters recede. And if you can't hold on for any other reason, hold on just to spite anyone who sought to break you. Breathe as an act of rebellion. Breathe as an act of defiance. Breathe as a prayer to the Divine within you.

MERRY CHRISTMAS, YA FILTHY ANIMALS!

I LOVE YOU!

136

The other day I realized that he both no longer exists *and* he still exists — because I do. Because my son does. Every breath I take is because he existed. Every time I stand up for someone I do so because he existed. Every time I love and rage and support and walk away, I do so because he existed. I ache because of his loss *and* he is not lost. The ones we lost are gone *and* they are always present. To live within the cognitive dissonance of grief is to live within the eye of a paradox so great it may take us our entire lifetimes to unravel it. Such is the price of love.

137

My therapist: I've noticed that you bounce back quicker and easier than you used to — you're becoming stronger all the time. All of the work you've been doing is showing.

Me, suddenly crying because of what she said, "Well . . . see that . . . clearly you don't know what you're talking about . . . "

She starts laughing.

Me, sniffling, " . . . fucking quack . . . "

And then she started laughing *really* hard.

We both did.

138

An interesting paradox of my emotional and spiritual growth is my lack of interest in always being the bigger person. Some days being the bigger person is essential to my feelings of peace and expansion and grace. Some days being the bigger person is a result of years of Buddhist study and training; of my desire to be an agent of good in this world, a *Bodhisattva*. Some days, being the bigger person is an intrinsic part of my being a highly spiritually evolved human being.

And some days you can go fuck yourself.

Growth is so awesome.

139

A friend just asked what it was that always got me through life's troubles in the past and I said my dad, and when she nodded somberly and asked, "So, what gets you through now?" I answered, "Well, it's not like he's gone."

Wait. Say *what?*

Y'all.

I didn't even expect that to come out of my . . . mouth? Spirit? I just know that in that moment I'd never before been so certain he's still with me in some form, protecting me like always, supporting me like always, loving me like always.

I actually said, *"It's not like he's gone."*

What?! I've been mourning his death for three and a half YEARS and in that instant, in that moment, it was like he was just in another room.

How unbelievably fucking strange is that?

190

Sometimes the fact that he's dead makes me feel so old, and then sometimes it's like I'm six and I'm in my room reading my books quietly, waiting for my daddy to get home from work.

Any minute now.

He'll be here any minute.

191

I don't hate Father's Day anymore.

I mean, don't get me wrong, it makes me even more sad than I already am that he's not here. And I'm a raging inferno of envy when I see those of you spending it with your dads (I don't begrudge you that joy, I'm just jealous. It's the simple truth).

But I don't hate Father's Day this year.

I was SO lucky. So incredibly lucky. I had a man in my life who literally ran into a burning building four times to save strangers' lives — do you have any idea the lengths he went to in life for *me*? The care and love and support he gave me every. single. day of my life? Do you know what it's like to never once wonder if your father loves you? To know deep down in the marrow of your bones that you are the most important person in the Universe to someone? To know that no matter how far a fall from grace you experienced, that there was someone who would pick you up, dust you off, curse you the fuck out for doing that dumb shit, then set you up for a successful bounce back in every way they could? I had a father who taught me to be a fearsome warrior for those who are silenced. He taught me to be a loving and generous person to the people who matter most. He taught me how to have ice in my stare and how to set the world on fire with the flames on my tongue.

He taught me how to be Issa.

I was the luckiest little girl in the whole wide world.

I still am.

192

I'm sitting here in what I can only describe as shock.

It's early morning and I've just woken my kid up for school. I'm in the kitchen washing dishes in the sink, and out of the corner of my eye I see someone walk about a fourth of the way past the kitchen and then turn around again and go back the way they came. I kept washing the dishes, not thinking anything of it, because I initially thought it was my kid going back for his robe. And then I realized: I hadn't heard any sounds. If he had reached for his robe, which is hung up on a hook behind his door, I would've heard the hinges on his door creak as he closed the door to access the hook. I stood there waiting to hear the door creaking, hearing nothing. I put the sponge down and turn off the water. I go into his bedroom. He's still asleep in his bed. It then dawns on me that I also heard no footsteps on this extremely creaky floor because he didn't make them. I ask him if he had gotten up and he mumbles a sleepy, "No."

My brain is trying to come up with rational explanations. I have none.

Except. Uhm . . .

Hi, Daddy.

193

Of all the many things I learned from my father, the one I'm most grateful for is how to be brave. I may never have to be as brave as a man running back into a burning building four times to save the lives of strangers, but I'm brave enough to run into the fire of life over and over again to save myself, and for that I have him to thank.

Your kid is okay, Daddy. Look at what an amazing job you did.

199

I think we could all do a much better job of allowing people their sadness.

If I say that the thought of ever getting married without my father walking me down the aisle breaks my heart into a million pieces, sit with that with me. Don't try to make me "feel better" by suggesting that my son can walk me down the aisle. My son is not my father. I don't want my child to do that. That was my daddy's job to do. That does not make me feel at all "better" about my dead father.

I know people mean well, and they just don't want to see me hurting, and I really do appreciate the intent. The thing is, whether it's my sadness — or your discomfort with another's sadness — saying things like that invalidates the feelings being expressed. It causes people to not talk to you about the weighty things. The painful things. The real things. They grow vines out of their hands clutching to deeply-rooted pain no one seems to want to acknowledge. It's painful and it's lonely. It's not at all helpful or kind.

So, instead of rushing in to try to "fix" a feeling that doesn't need to be fixed (just honored), perhaps a gentle, "I can definitely understand that," would do. Everyone is grieving something, whether it be the loss of a loved one, a relationship, a homeland, an ideal. Everyone is grieving something. The paradox of this is that if we can sit with each other through that grief instead of rushing to "fix" it, the painful parts ebb away much quicker. They'll come back again, for sure, because grief doesn't end, but at least the waves become less of a tsunami and more surfable.

Let's just sit with each other through the hard parts, okay? Sometimes holding space and bearing witness to each other's pain is the most loving thing we can do. Sometimes a simple, "I hear you," is all we really need.

145

"Do you think Grandpa has reincarnated already?"

"No, I highly doubt it. As protective as he was in life, I'm pretty sure he's still around us now, protecting and supporting us like he did in life. He'll probably be here for as long as I'm alive, and maybe even for as long as you're alive."

"Is that fair? Shouldn't he be able to move on again?"

"Knowing your grandpa the way I did, there's nowhere else he'd rather be than by our sides. He'll move on when he's ready."

"Okay."

September, man. After my kid's birthday on the eighth it's all downhill from there.

196

Tomorrow is 9/11.

I wish I could go to a place where that day doesn't exist.

197

My kid's talking to a friend on the phone who overhears a woman's loud scream from the show I was watching.

"Oh, it's nothing. Just some movie my mom is watching."

"I don't know, some ghost movie, probably. She's always watching something scary."

"No, she even watches those things at night alone in her room after I go to bed. She's not afraid of that stuff. My mom isn't afraid of anything."

If only he knew.

If only he knew I'm afraid of *everything*.

All the time.

Especially without my dad here.

Well . . . Everything except maybe ghosts.

My heart is filled with them.

198

Laughing and shaking my head at this memory:

My dad and I were in Puerto Rico once on vacation when I was 30 years old and we were sitting in the hotel's huge hot tub on the beach. It's me, my dad, and three or four men. I got out to use the bathroom, and when I got back my dad was sitting there, alone, looking furious.

"Oh, God. What happened? What did you do?"

"Dirty muthafuckas!"

"Daddy. What. Did. You. Do?"

"When you got out they all said disgusting shit about you in your bikini, and how I was an 'inspiration' for getting a hot, young thing like you. So, I told them you were my *DAUGHTER*, and then proceeded to curse their dirty asses the fuck out. That's what the fuck I did."

Me, sighing, "I'm gonna go get a Piña Colada."

I shook my head and laughed all the way to the bar.

199

Someone just asked me if I've seen my father since he passed, and I said a couple of months ago I saw something right outside of my kitchen that I *think* was my dad, but since what I saw was in my periphery I couldn't be sure it was him.

They asked if I would want to see his spirit or if I'd be afraid. I told them the only thing I'd be afraid of was him telling me that he was disappointed in me. Disappointed in the nothing I've done with my life. Disappointed in the nothing I've done with all of the supposed potential I have. Disappointed in the failure I am after all he invested in me for forty-two years. I'm afraid he isn't proud of me because other than giving him his grandson I feel like I have nothing to be proud of.

This month, man. It'll be four years on the 21st and it doesn't get any better. Not really. Not ever.

150

I hate 9/11. I really do.

I tried to be okay today. I really did. But I'm not. I'm not okay. I was told by someone that I needed to get over his loss and let go already. That I'll be stuck and incapable of truly moving forward with my life if I didn't find a way to stop grieving and let go. Maybe they're right. Four years is a long time to not be okay. Thing is, I honestly don't know how to let go. To get over it. To move on. They said I'm going to block any blessings coming my way in life if I continue to wallow in the pain of grief. That I have to want to be healed more than I want to feel the pain of his loss, or else my life is going to be nothing but a density of gloom.

Maybe they're right. Maybe they are.

All I know is, my father isn't here because he chose to not only save people from those burning towers, but because of the days afterwards looking for survivors — and then the weeks afterwards pulling bodies out of the rubble — with inadequate respiratory protection. He died because of something evil and terrifying. He died because of inadequate protection. He died because of something I'll never understand, something I'm reminded of on the world stage year after year after painful year.

Ten days from now, back in 2015, I walked into an emergency room with my father's dead body in it, and I screamed and screamed and screamed. A part of me is still screaming. And I don't think there's any getting over that.

151

I watched a video of Serena Williams as a child being defended against a reporter by her father. It immediately made me think, "I had a father like that. It's why I'm considered 'difficult' and 'too outspoken' and 'challenging.' It's also why I will never, ever choke and die on my own voice to appease others."

My dad did a lot 'wrong' while I was growing up because of his own painful upbringing, but teaching me to look people straight in the eyes and tell them to go fuck themselves if they tried to belittle me is something he definitely did right.

It's true. My daddy raised a warrior. Even when I'm at my weakest.

Especially then.

152

The most profound grace I've been shown in my life is by the friends who didn't take my isolating when in a depressive episode triggered by profound grief personally, who have forgiven my abandoning them as I nurse myself back to some semblance of health, and who have welcomed me and our friendship back with love as if I was never gone to begin with.

Friends like that are rare and priceless. You have no idea how disorienting and lonesome it is to emerge from a depressive episode and the people you love are hurt that they've been abandoned by you and are nowhere to be found. There is no one cheering you on for making it through. There is only a trail of broken relationships and hurt feelings. It reifies your experience of being profoundly alone. That sense of being alone in the world can have dire consequences for someone who is grappling with their mental health.

If you are a friend who loves and supports someone who has struggled with profound grief and/or mental illness, thank you. You save lives and you don't even realize it.

And if you can be that kind of friend to someone today, please — *please* — do so. I guarantee you'll both be better for it.

153

When you wake up from a dream (I don't remember many dreams. I have maybe twenty or thirty dreams remembered in total my entire forty-plus years on this earth, so to remember any at all is strange for me), in which your father tells you he wants you to find love again because he doesn't want you all alone in the world like you are right now, and you realize that now you have to posthumously disown him, because there's no way you're getting back out there again.

Absolutely not, old man.

No.

159

Another Christmas is coming without him.

I thought I was doing okay, but the closer to Christmas it gets the less okay I am.

Maybe okay is something I won't ever be. Not really. Not all the way through.

The trauma of profound loss is so untidy, isn't it? It refuses to be resolved at the end of the Hallmark holiday special.

There are so many people out there right now trying to be so very brave.

Please, be kind as much as you can, my loves.

So many of us out here are mourning heartrending losses that will never be fully alleviated by time.

155

Whenever someone met my dad there was a moment when you could see the light go on in their heads and they'd inevitably say, "Now I totally get you. Now I understand exactly why you are the person you are."

I'm really sad that whoever I've met since his passing, and whoever I meet going forward in my life, will never "get me" as completely as those who knew my dad.

Living past the point that the biggest part of you dies is some hard shit, y'all. So very, very hard.

Sending my love to those in the thick of their own "holiday" grief. I get it. I'm sorry.

156

Remembering after my dad came out of intubation and sedation for the first ten days he was in ICU. Remembering how every time I'd leave the room or hospital and come back, he'd have a new story from an ICU team member about what I did while he was under, and when I'd come back into his room the man who was courageous enough to run into a burning building four times to save complete strangers would look at me and start to tear up, telling me how amazing I was, what a blessing I was to him, how proud he was of how I fought for him, and you would think that those memories would make me feel good, but alas, that doesn't seem to be how grief works.

There's a small child in my heart that thinks, maybe if I hadn't handled everything so well, maybe if I hadn't been so strong, maybe he wouldn't have chosen to leave. Maybe he thought he could go because it looked like I would be alright in the end.

I'm not alright. And it never ends.

Don't let anyone put a time limit on your expressions of grief.

Grief is the price you pay for love.

157

My father told someone something once that's never left me.

Someone said that they were angry at their adult child because they mostly seemed to call when they needed something. My dad replied, "It's been the greatest honor of my life to be the one person my daughter thinks of calling when she's in need."

That's the kind of person who raised me. That's how I'm raising my kid.

No, I don't tolerate disrespect. Anyone who has seen me with my kid knows this.

No, I don't tolerate ingratitude. I have no desire to raise and let loose yet another selfish, self-absorbed, immature human being into this world.

But being a parent doesn't stop at eighteen. Or at twenty-one, for that matter. And you wanted that baby, right?

That means when they're gay. That means when they're trans. That means when they're goths. That means when they're metal heads. That means when they're mentally ill. That means when they're broke. Sometimes, that means when they're grown up, too.

No, don't enable your kids to depend on you forever. Yes, raise children to be as self-sufficient as possible. No, don't raise your kids to live off of you for the rest of their lives. But some of you act like just because you suffered without support as young adults your kids should, too, so that they can become strong like you.

That ain't it, Chief.

You think the wealthy leave their kids to sink or swim? You think that hundreds of years of financial privilege among certain economic classes of people hasn't been cemented for future generations by the willingness of their parents to invest in their children and their futures by helping them every way they can, whenever they can? You think in these terrifying economic times, with Ivy League graduates living out of tents under freeways, you think self-sufficiency is a static thing? A thing that remains once it's attained? Because there is a whole slew of people in this world who did "all the right things" and "got all the right degrees" and "pulled themselves up by their own bootstraps," only to have to season those same boots with packets of ketchup stolen from the local McDonald's in order to have something to eat that night. All that separates you from the streets isn't your own tenacity — it's community. Support. Who will hold you safe when things fall apart? For too many people, the answer is no one.

When times are hard for our kids, no matter the reason, no matter their age, it's important they know they can always come to us and we will always help them find a solution.

As parents, it's our greatest honor to be the ones they think of calling when they are in need.

158

I know a lot of us are afraid. Afraid of loss. Afraid of betrayal. Afraid of breaking. But earlier this morning I left a comment on a friend's Facebook post and it's been rattling around in my head all day. It was in response to an amazing post she reposted by someone who claimed his victory for the past year was not having let the slings and arrows of misfortune break him. And while I honor that sentiment and I honor anyone who has been through the gauntlet and did not break, I, of course, had a different take. I'll share my comment with you:

"Oh, I broke. Since 2015. Since putting Daddy in a hole in the ground. Since everything that happened afterwards. Oh, I broke. I broke, and I broke, and I broke. But I didn't die. So, when my pleas to slip into nothingness weren't granted, I mended myself. For each time I was broken. Over and over again. And I'll be mending myself for the rest of my life, I'm sure. But I'm stronger than what sought to kill me. And that's what I take with me going forward. That I can break and not die. That I can break and still be a light to others. That I can break and still be whole. That's all I got."

You can break, my loves. You *will* break. If life has anything to do with it, you will break over and over and over again.

You can mend yourselves, my loves. You can. If love has anything to do with it, you will be able to mend yourself over and over and over again.

To not risk breaking is to not risk actually living. To be afraid of breaking is to be blinded to your innate power for healing yourself. For growth.

Some of the best people in life have been broken to bits, burnt to ashes, and left for dust. Then, somehow, we gather our ashes, add the Water of Life, and bring ourselves back from the brink of death.

Risk being broken, my loves. Risk it. Because Life will break you anyway. Because when it's all said and done, none of us get out of this sans scars. None of us. And those scars are the roadmaps of our personal evolution.

"Risk" is clearly going to be the word that threads through my year. I'm almost foolish enough to look forward to how it shows up in my life.

Almost.

159

On the train. A dad and his daughter sitting across from us. Their bond is palpable. Dad gets up right before their stop. Leans against the door. Opens his arms wide. She walks into them smiling. He holds her for a second. Doors open. They walk out. I try to stop my eyes from what they are about to do. They do it anyway. I wipe them before my kid can see. We get up and walk out of the train after them. I feel light-headed. My stomach is nauseated. It's been four years, I tell myself. Stop this. Get it together. But there is no together. There is no time. There is only the chasm that swallows you whole when you least expect it. The chasm is beyond time. The chasm is always.

There is no time.

There is no better.

There's only always.

Just like that love.

160

One of the most difficult things I've learned, as a Buddhist and as a person who has had her share of tragedies and traumas in life, is that if you sit with the pain you are feeling, if you fully feel every shard, that pain moves on of its own accord. Sure, it may come back again, but it stays for slightly less time when it does. It feels slightly less sharp.

I think back to people who have accused me of "wallowing" in my pain and ruefully laugh. They have spent their entire lives avoiding their pain and are sleepwalking through their emotions. They have a limited understanding of "reality" and an even more limited ability to engage with and navigate it. They fumble their emotional needs and the emotional needs of others when things are difficult. They all have a severely limited range in managing the full breadth of their human emotions.

As painful as it can be sometimes, I sit with reality. I allow it to be as it is. I may fumble and fight it a little at first because I am only human after all. Eventually, though, I just sit with it. I feel it. All of it. I cry. I scream. I write. I sit with it some more. I cry some more. I sit.

The ability to sit with my pain has paradoxically been a source of strength for me. Trust me when I tell you, there will be times when you won't be able to run from your pain, and if you haven't learned how to process it, it will either consume your life or you will sublimate it into socially acceptable self-destruction like too much drinking or numbing out with TV and social media. Learning to sit with your pain, to acknowledge its existence, to validate its rawness, and to then allow it to leave of its own accord, is one of the most important things you can do for yourself. For the people you love. For us all. Because unhealed people hurt the world around them, and you can't heal the pain until you sit with it.

161

That liminal space between who you were and who you are becoming can feel really tough to be in. You're tempted to go backwards to the comfort of what you know, even if it wasn't working for you, and you're scared to walk into what is coming because of a primal fear of the dark. Of the unknown.

I know. I get it.

Let's just keep taking one small step at a time. Personal transformation, growth, and healing are a marathon, not a sprint. Take a rest if needed, but keep going — because what if the best version of yourself and your life is just around the bend of that dark path through the near-impenetrable forest of fear? What if who you are now isn't a sum total of your past — what if who you are now is your future calling you to it?

Just remember: I know you can sometimes feel all alone in this space, but you're not. I'm in those woods, too. And while we may not be out of them yet, we're closer to the clearing than we've ever been. Just one more step. And then just one more. We can do this.

162

I, and this isn't hyperbole here, haven't had nude toenails in decades. I always keep a pedicure and the reason is simple: getting a pedicure has consistently been the one thing I've done since my twenties as "self-care," even when things were at their worst.

Well, for obvious reasons, I haven't gone to get a pedicure since before the pandemic. And I hate doing my own feet because that doesn't feel like self-care, it just feels like more work. Yesterday I had to take off the 1 millimeter of nail polish I had left on my toes because it was just ridiculous at this point, and I just now glanced down at my completely naked feet and gasped.

These are my father's feet.

I always knew I had his hands, but . . . I have his feet, too.

All these years with polish on and I hadn't even realized.

I literally walk with my father's feet. The same feet that ran into that building and saved those lives that horrific day. The same feet that marched in military boots for his country in the late 1960s even after his sergeant and fellow Marines taunted and beat him for being a *"funny-looking nigger."* The same feet that walked him through my door whenever I needed him for even the smallest thing.

I'm looking at these feet and I'm beyond shocked. How did I not know this? How did I never realize that these were his exact same feet?

I'm stunned.

This was a reminder — so that I always remember who I am and who I come from as I walk this earth without him here.

May I continue to walk these feet into a life he would be proud of. I'll never be the hero he was, but I hope to continue his legacy of standing up to oppression, protecting the "little guy," and loving my people so thoroughly that they feel it long after I'm gone.

163

I found an old post on Facebook today:

"My dad drives me crazy. C.R.A.Z.Y. Like, mini-psychotic-break-crazy. He rarely understands me, he rarely validates me, and he rarely makes me feel as if EVERYTHING I do isn't open for constructive criticism. BUT. Without his too-often support I wouldn't be able to freelance and be a mostly stay-at-home single mom for my son. He immediately fights my objections to his old-school macho bullshit, but *always* considers it afterwards, and clearly implements my opinions/viewpoints into how he approaches me thereafter. He loves and dotes on my son in a way that fills my son with feeling extremely special and important. He and I may never see eye-to-eye, but he has always, *always* made me feel as if I am the most important human being in his life, and that he loves me unconditionally; no matter what I do or don't do. He's getting older, and is very ill because of the effects of 9/11 and his role as a first responder. I fight with him less. I love him more. I thank God for the standard he's set, for me and for my son. I'm a 40-year-old Daddy's girl, and I wouldn't change that for the world."

If only I knew that less than two years later he'd be gone. I wonder if I would've done anything differently.

Today I read some old text messages from my father. I haven't been able to do that in over five years. I've tried to read his messages before and they would just leave me gutted, so I stopped reading them years ago.

Today was different. Today when I read them, he didn't feel "gone." Even though he hasn't shown up on my sofa, drinking his coffee and offering a scathing indictment of the world's multitude of sins, somehow I know he's here. He's here. Those messages went from a symbol of his absence to a reminder that he never left me.

I think maybe I'm finally healing.

169

My son became a man tonight.

There was a mouse in my bathroom and I hid in my room after having him go in with a broom to flush it out.

I'm so proud of him. He did it without even blinking. He even made fun of me for being a grown woman "afraid of a hamster," just like my dad would've. Daddy would've been so proud, too. So proud.

I am not, however, proud of myself. I sacrificed my son to save myself.

I am ashamed and disgraced.

I will do it again in a heartbeat, though.

#QuokkaMom

165

Today is Valentine's Day, and it isn't being single that makes me sad, it's being fatherless. The year after he died was the first Valentine's Day in my entire adult life that I didn't receive a dozen long-stemmed roses delivered to me thanking me for being his kid and telling me that he loved me.

A dozen long-stemmed roses. From him. Always from him.

I miss you, Daddy.

166

This week's discovery during therapy was that despite not even seeing it, much less giving myself credit for it, my growth these past six months has been pretty substantial. I'm very slowly taking over four decades of negative conditioning, repeated trauma, and the maladaptive coping mechanisms I've used to manage it all, and am moving the needle ever so slightly toward healing and growth. It was almost suddenly obvious to both my therapist and me: there is growth here. I'm nowhere near where I'd like to be, but I've been swimming through shards of glass for a long time, and some days it's nice to realize, even if just for a fleeting moment, how amazing I have been through it all. How much care I've shown myself even when it was exceedingly hard to do. How much I am willing to grow even when it hurts. How much I am still able to love despite the scar tissue that threatens to rob me of all feeling. How I am still here. That I am still here.

I wanted to remind you that sometimes when you feel stuck, you're actually in the middle of growing. In the middle of shedding. In the middle of becoming. It's not easy, but miracles seldom are. And if I can be certain of anything it's that I am a motherfucking miracle.

Try to remember that you are, too.

One of the things that happens after a while is that you go from feeling nothing but their absence to feeling them everywhere. It's a gradual thing, but eventually you realize that you, your life, and everything you see in the world has been filled with so much of them that there is no absence. They are everywhere you are. You never stop longing to have them here in the physical, to hear their voice, to hear them say, "I'm proud of you," but now you hear it in your mind as it recovers. In your spirit as it rebounds. In your heart as it beats.

Beat: "I'm proud of you."

Beat: "I'm proud of you."

Beat: "I'm so proud of you."

Oh, the joy in that realization. The love that keeps your heart beating long after you wished it would've stopped when theirs did. It's so excruciating and beautiful at the same time.

Hang on, okay? I know it all hurts and I know there are days you want to pack it all in but hold on. I don't know when you'll get to this place I'm in but you will. You will. Just please, hang on until then.

167

"This isn't you. This isn't who you are. This is just a maladaptive coping mechanism you learned, and you can unlearn it. Don't identify with it and choose differently whenever possible. You are not your coping mechanisms, you are your awareness. You are the person who wants to grow from where you've been stuck. You're okay. You got this."

Just wanted to share what I've been telling myself lately when I find that I am beating myself up for something, in case it's a helpful internal script you can use for yourself.

168

It's taken me almost thirty years to understand that depression has been a way my brain has tried to soothe me from the hyper-vigilance of trauma and high anxiety. When your nervous system has been turned all the way on and all the way UP because of trauma and the resulting hyper-vigilance, the subsequent depression is a maladaptive way for your brain to "calm down." Going forward, any prominent stressor in your life tends to be followed by a precipitous crash to "help" you come down from intense trauma/agitation, and if you have years and years and *years* of this dynamic, your nervous system just thinks this is "normal." And that's what the cycle becomes. Normal.

Depression can have multiple causes, and that can be as individual as a person's fingerprints. There is no "one size fits all" cause or treatment. Each person has their own story they are living. Just know that if you've experienced periods of profound depression in your life, you are literally an expression of the indefatigable resilience of the human psyche, and there is nothing wrong with you.

There. Is. Nothing. Wrong. With. You.

You are an amazing example of how hard our minds work to save us from harm and keep us as whole as possible after trauma. Even suicidal ideation is just a way the brain tries to soothe us. Anyone who has ever courted suicidal thoughts will tell you, we didn't want to die, we just wanted the pain to stop. Our minds, even in that most terrible "solution," were simply trying to soothe our pain. It's our job to recognize those thoughts as symptoms, not as an answer. It's our job to get help when we need it. But most of all, it's our job to remember that we are incredible survivors worthy of high praise. We've run through the jungles of life with tigers growling at our heels. Sometimes they've even sunken their teeth into us, making us fear for our lives, and scarring us forever. And yet here we still are. Here we stand. We are glorious and broken and oh-so-beautifully, terribly human. And that's okay. Get help to develop survival methods that are no longer maladaptive, yes. But please, remember: There is nothing wrong with you.

You are your own hero. You are likely a hero to many others as well and may not even realize it. You are not your worst thoughts about yourself. You, my love, are fucking amazing.

You truly are.

169

Hi.

Fuck people's "best intentions" for you.

No one gets to decide what's best for you. Their opinion of you and your journey has nothing to do with you and is clouded by their own perspectives.

Sometimes other's feedback is valuable. Sometimes someone is giving you news you can actually use. Evaluate it accordingly.

Mostly it's just manipulation, though.

You'd be surprised how many people want you to "move on from mourning" because it makes *them* uncomfortable to deal with grief, not because they are really, truly, honestly worried about you.

Be a kind person, operate from integrity, and do you. Take however long you need to heal. Everyone around you will adjust — or not. That's on them.

Okay. That was it.

Bye.

170

I just now understand why I cry when I hear my kid sing and play his guitar.

My dad got a lot right. One of the things he got terribly wrong was discouraging me from pursuing my dream of being a singer because I was "too smart to be a struggling artist." He encouraged and invested in my academics growing up and that was that.

He crushed me when he did that.

Giving Theo the gift of learning an instrument and using his singing voice is a way for me to right that karmic wrong. Just writing that is making me cry.

I can't undo the loss of my dream, but I can make sure that whatever dream my kid has, no matter how small nor how "impractical," will be fully supported and invested in by me.

That's all I can do now. It will be enough somehow.

171

I was offered a session with a person who can speak with the dead who comes highly recommended by someone who had a session with them and was blown away by the details that came up, details that no one but her and the deceased could've possibly known. I declined because my first thought was that I didn't want to hear my dad tell me how disappointed he is in me.

Therapy is going fine — thanks for asking.

172

I was missing my dad really hard and then my kid and I walked past a hotel while walking the dog and the hotel loudspeaker started playing *"I'll Be Around"* by The Spinners, a song my Daddy loved. And whew. Silly me. I keep forgetting he hasn't gone any damn where.

He's right here.

Love never dies.

173

One of the best things about everything I've gone through, especially in the last few years, is how proud I am of myself for how I've handled it all. Even when I messed up and took a backward step or two — that, too, was a part of the growth process. I haven't always been proud of myself because I've allowed others to dictate that my self-pride be predicated upon external accomplishments, but man-oh-man have I so much to be proud of internally. My commitment to doing the internal work necessary for my growth as a human, as a parent, and as a spiritual being has consistently shown up for me when I most needed it, and I am so damn proud of Issa for that. Y'all. She is fucking amazing. It brings tears to my eyes as I write this to think of how much she has grown, and how much hard work she's put into that growth. She deserves all good things in life. She really does.

Are there ways in which you have grown that you are proud of? If not, could you be overlooking them because you are looking to external accomplishments to be proud of instead of the far more important work of internal growth that could be your source of pride? Could there be small steps made toward immense growth that you refuse to see? Start looking within, my loves. It is there that you will meet yourself fully.

179

I read somewhere today that it's not about "releasing" (or "letting go" of) our shitty inner voices. It's about offering those voices compassion while also not believing them — and I find that to be so very true. That has been a game changer for me. When I not only made a conscious effort not to talk to myself like I was a piece of shit for whatever I was getting "wrong" (not letting go of grief in an "appropriate" amount of time, not being where I wanted to be in life by this age, for *whatever*), but also recognized that the voice saying those things was a part of me that needed attention and compassion as well, a lot changed for me internally.

If you're beating yourself up for the stuckness caused by beating yourself up, well, that just doesn't make sense, does it? No, it doesn't. It took me a long time to figure that one out. Beating myself up for how long it was taking me to "stop grieving" never changed a single thing.

Interestingly, this brings to mind the notion of "letting go of the ego" or the spiritual goal of "ego death." I know those are buzz words commonly attributed to Buddhism, as well as to the "New Age Movement," but allow me to tell you that trying to kill the ego doesn't work and does no good. There is nothing wrong with having an ego, you just have to learn not to lead with it. Allow it to inform you of your environment, allow it to create healthy boundaries for you, allow it to work *for* you, but this impossible ideal of killing your ego and operating from pure spirit is a hindrance to the real work of integration. If we were meant to be pure spiritual beings we wouldn't have incarnated. What we are meant, at least in these human incarnations, is to operate from spirit *and* to use ego to navigate this earthly plane in a way that is healthy and symbiotic with those around us. People venerate the isolated monk but it's easy to be peaceful when you don't have to deal with the egoic nature of other humans. The real work is in relating to others, navigating conflict, and balancing spirit with ego. All else is folly.

175

I walked out of my building and there was a car parked out in front blasting what at first sounded like my father singing. Stunned, I stopped to really listen to what it was that I was hearing, and realized that it was "*Kiss And Say Goodbye*" by The Manhattans playing, a song I'd heard my dad sing at least a hundred times. I didn't know whether to tear up or smile. So, I did both.

When I came back home, I found the song, and played it and sang along.

And sobbed.

It's been five and a half years.

This grief shit never fucking ends.

176

I read a piece written by someone who feels embarrassed in the summer when she wears short sleeves because her self-harm scars show. The thing I'd like to point out is that self-harm or "cutting" isn't just a physical act. I've been an emotional cutter my whole life. What does that look like? Self-flagellation. Obsessive rumination over the past. Self-blame for things that were in no way within my control. Eating things that were unhealthy for me in huge amounts to stuff down the pain. Drinking too much. Staying in relationships longer than I should've (which is ironic because I'm known for leaving relationships super quick if I see red flags, but the truth is I saw them long before I left and didn't leave out of a misplaced sense of "loyalty" to others instead of to myself). Playing and staying small in life. Constantly choosing people who hurt me and then using that to not trust myself again in the future. Keeping promises to everyone outside of me but seldom keeping promises to myself. The list goes on.

If you find that you have a history of doing these things, you probably have unhealed trauma you're carrying around. Getting trauma-informed therapy has been one of the most loving and important things I've ever done for myself. Please, get the support you need to help recover from the things that have harmed you in your life. You deserve relief. You deserve to heal, inside and out.

177

Me, messing something up: Ugh! I'm so damn stupid!

My kid, from the other room: So, I'm not allowed to insult myself but you're allowed to do that? You're not stupid, Mom. You just made a mistake.

Thought #1: If I could just be as kind to myself as I am to others maybe one day I'd be okay.

Thought #2: You're teaching him to be mean to himself just like your dad taught you by being so mean to himself.

Thought #3: No, you've corrected him when he's done that enough so he knew to correct you when you did it. He's okay. He won't be anywhere near as broken as you are.

Being a parent is the hardest thing I've ever loved.

Being my father's daughter is a close second.

178

I am a haunted house. My left knee creaks like an old door when I sit, the floorboards and I groan when I get up from meditations, and there are ghosts everywhere. It is a house filled with scary stories, profound loss, and unbelievable pain. It is a house filled with treasures stuffed into unused drawers and old closets. It has a sturdy foundation and good bones, but it needs repair and a lot of love. It lives on the corner of Hope and Sorrow. It is beautiful in its deterioration. It will never be what it was, but it can be made new again, too. Slowly. With time. With love. With care. This haunted house will always have its ghosts, but they will no longer scare. They will feel like the quiet joy of an afternoon breeze floating through an open window, whispering, "You mattered. You were so loved. We were so happy to see you live."

179

One of the most important things I've learned in the trauma work I've done is something I'd bet good money some of you need to hear:

You are not lazy. Your lack of self-motivation is a trauma response.

180

I cried today as I recounted a moment in which my father, yet again, did something deeply loving and generous for me, and the person said, "I'm sorry."

Let me tell you what I told them:

"I'm not. Tears aren't anything to be afraid of, you know? Right now they are just liquid gratitude. I was so lucky. I was *so* damn lucky, you know? To be loved that much? It's a blessing that has lived on past his physical body. It will live on through my kid. I don't have enough tears for how grateful I am. It's okay. Tears are okay. Don't be afraid of my tears. Or your own."

181

I bumped into a neighbor who has lived in this building for as long as I have (thirty-eight years). He told me a story about sitting out front in my dad's car having a conversation with him, and he told me that my dad said the following:

"She told me off today because I told her she was gaining too much weight. She told me that was none of my business and I needed to keep that mess to myself. I got upset and told her I was worried about her health and she told me to go worry about something else because I was a cop not a damn doctor. Can you believe that?"

"I don't know why I argue with my daughter; she's smarter than I am and even more stubborn. And let me tell you something: there's no one more stubborn than me. Well, except for her."

"When my daughter decided to call off her wedding she thought I'd be upset with her because she was pregnant, but I was so proud of her. I knew they weren't right for each other and I knew she'd be a great mom anyway. It's not like she'll do this alone as long as I'm alive, anyway."

September 11th is in two weeks. He died on September 21st. I can already feel it all creeping up inside me.

182

The 20-year anniversary of 9/11 is doing me in. All of these documentaries. I find them disgusting. I can't help but wonder how the families of Holocaust survivors feel when they see yet another documentary on Dachau or Auschwitz advertised. I know it's important for the next generation, to help people to never forget. I just can't help feeling like there is a voyeuristic feeling to them. Like how humans love to slow down as they pass a fatal accident — both wanting and also not wanting to see the bloodied corpses in front of them. Those corpses that have human beings who will spend the rest of their lives mourning them. We say "never forget" but for some of us, there is a constant remembering. There will never be a forgetting. We don't have that luxury.

183

Here's one of the things about grief I know to be true: In order not to get stuck in the more painful places grief can take you, you have to paradoxically feel every bit of the pain grief brings.

Running from the pain won't help you.

I've had people tell me that the way I've processed my grief around my dad's death is "unhealthy" because "I'm still there." Meanwhile, these people drink too much alcohol, smoke too much weed, and/or check out with TV and social media to the point of complete avoidance. Still. Many years after the death of their loved one.

You can't heal by avoiding healing. And you can't heal by avoiding the pain.

I'm good, y'all. I hurt, and I hurt deeply, but I'm also healing in ways some people can't even begin to grasp.

The only way out is through. Through the loss, through the regrets, through the pain.

I promise you, if you're brave enough to face it all, you'll be brave enough to face life itself. There is no life without death. There is no joy without the pain of loss. It is the very fabric of life. We are all but one moment away from our own mortality. That is okay. It's as it should be. Face it all with as much courage as you can muster, because loss is going to happen regardless. Better to run toward it than to run away from it. Better to walk this earth as a warrior than as a deserter. Better to feel it all than to go numb. You were born into this existence to feel. Don't throw that gift away.

189

Six years ago today.

Six years ago today I walked into the emergency room of a hospital, praying that he was okay. I walked in and begged to be told what was going on, but the nurse at the desk, rather dismissively, said I had to wait to speak to the doctor, and just like in that scene from *Terms of Endearment*, I banged on the desk and screamed to be heard. "WHERE IS MY FATHER??? SOMEONE TELL ME WHERE MY FATHER IS!!!" As I felt myself start to unravel, as my brain told me that the only reason they wouldn't tell me what was going on is if he were already dead, I saw a doctor run over to me. I ran to meet him and asked, "Is he alive?" only to have the doctor look at me with sadness-shaped eyes and shake his head, "No."

No.

When he walked me into the room where my father lay, dead, and I saw my daddy lying there, still intubated, looking like he was merely asleep, a sound came out of me I had never heard before. I know now that it's what a heart breaking apart sounds like. I know now that it's what pain from inside your very soul sounds like. I know now that it was the sound of little Issa, dying.

Six years ago today I lost my father forever. Don't tell me "he's still with me." I don't want to hear that today. Today is the sixth anniversary of the day I saw my daddy lying on a gurney, dead. The sounds that came out of my broken heart as I held his hand for the very last time haunt me to this day.

I know he's spiritually with me. Today that's not enough. Today I honor that sometimes it's not enough.

Today I honor the grief that is the price you pay for an immensity of love. I pay it willingly. I will pay it until the end of my own days.

185

The days after 9/11 and 9/21 often leave me feeling sore, as if I ran full marathons for days on end. My feet may not be blistered, my skin chafed, my knees inflamed — but my swollen eyes give me away. The listlessness in my step betrays the heaviness of my bones. I have gone through the gauntlet, yet again. I have made it through. It was painful, yes. It was also a reminder. A reminder of the love I had. Of the constant support I had. A reminder that I was the most important person in the entire world to someone, and that they spent my whole life actively showing it.

His loss is a reminder that love is a risk, no matter what form it takes. His loss is a reminder that life can be excruciatingly painful.

If you're lucky.

186

Six years ago today I buried my father.

Some days it feels as if it's been decades since I've heard him call my name. Since I've heard him curse someone out (heh heh). Since I've heard him tell me he loves me.

It's been six years of feeling like I'm all alone in this world, swimming upstream in a hurricane.

Six years of finding my way in a world in which he no longer is alive.

Six years of staring into the abyss and sometimes wishing it would swallow me whole.

It's also been six years of healing.

Six years of growing stronger.

Six years of living in ever-anchoring integrity.

Six years of undoing unhealthy past conditioning.

Six years of learning to be kind and compassionate with myself.

Six years of learning how to show myself grace.

It's been the six hardest years of my life. For a while there in the beginning, I didn't think I'd make it to this day. For a while there I was a zombie, going through the motions of "life" for the benefit of my son.

Six years later and I've grown alive in ways that make me proud of Issa. This woman, y'all. She is a walking paradox. She is pain and ruin and healing and growth. I marvel at how she is still here, expanding, learning, loving. She is a miracle. She is a wonder.

She is her father's child.

May I continue to make him proud.

Acknowledgments

There is a larger memoir in me about my father's passing — and my gauntlet of a recovery from his loss — that I was writing at first, but it has taken too long to finish because of the depth of emotion I have to mine in order to get it on paper. Having chronicled my grief via Facebook posts, blog posts, published short pieces, and journal entries, I realized I already had a book about what transpired if I just took all of those words and put them together into book form. This is that book. Thank you to the friends who said it was a great idea when I first told them about it, and who reminded me that I already have all the words I could ever need.

To Deesha Philyaw, my Nettie, my sister from a thousand prior incarnations, thank you for your love, your support, and your faith in me as a writer. You have been such a gift to me in so many ways.

To Maria Emilia Vargas, my best friend, my rock, thank you for getting me through the toughest time of my life. I'd go through fire for you, but you already know that.

To Staci Jordan Shelton, thank you for your genuine friendship, your integrity, and your spiritual support. The people you coach are some of the luckiest people in the world.

To my family and friends, Kellye (Lollye) McMillion, Shandsmen Thomas, Deniz, Sibelle and Jayda Muttalip-Mejia, Amanda Isaacson, Hasani Blue, Lenée Voss, Gonzalo Garcia, Elizabeth Fletcher-Thomas, Angela Mack, and so many others my sieve of a brain is surely forgetting, thank you for being a part of my loving tribe.

And to my mother, Leila Rivera Reyes, without whom I wouldn't be here in so many ways, thank you for filling in the gaps, for being my scaffold when I most needed it, and for loving your grandson the way that you do. Theo and I wouldn't have gotten through that time in our lives without you.

About the Author

Issa M. Mas lives in New York City with her 14-year-old son, Theodore, and their dog, Jake. As a 20-year practicing Buddhist she brings a wealth of wisdom and loving kindness to the lives of others, but as an over 40-year native New Yorker her prolific use of profanity will never end. You can find her sporadically posted thoughts at www.issamas.com.